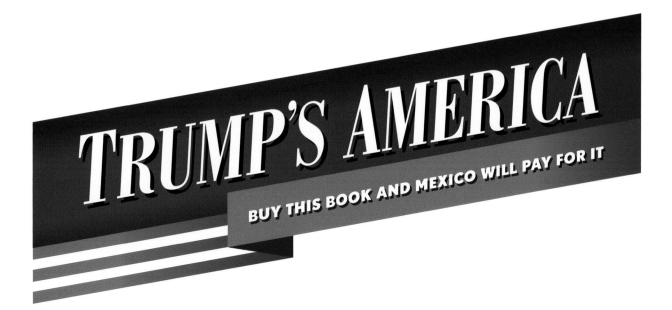

TRUMP'S AMERICA

BUY THIS BOOK AND MEXICO WILL PAY FOR IT

TRUMP'S AMERICA

BUY THIS BOOK AND MEXICO WILL PAY FOR IT

GALLERY BOOKS

New York London Toronto Sydney New Delhi

G

Gallery Books
An Imprint of Simon & Schuster, Inc.
1230 Avenue of the Americas
New York, NY 10020

Copyright © 2017 by Blaffo Industries
Published by arrangement with Micro-Publishing Media Inc.

First/This Gallery Books trade paperback edition February 2017

GALLERY BOOKS and colophon are registered trademarks of Simon & Schuster, Inc.

For information about special discounts for bulk purchases, please contact Simon & Schuster Special Sales at 1-866-506-1949 or business@simonandschuster.com

The Simon & Schuster Speakers Bureau can bring authors to your live event. For more information or to book an event contact the Simon & Schuster Speakers Bureau at 1-866-248-3049 or visit our website at www.simonspeakers.com.

Manufactured in the United States of America

10 9 8 7 6 5 4 3 2 1

Library of Congress Cataloging-in-Publication Data is available.

ISBN 978-1-5011-7267-0
ISBN 978-1-5011-7268-7 (ebook)

This work was previously published as *Trump's America: The Complete Loser's Guide*.

TRUMP'S AMERICA

BUY THIS BOOK AND MEXICO WILL PAY FOR IT

EDITOR-IN-CHIEF
Scott Dikkers

WRITERS AND EDITORS
Rosie Chevalier, Mike Clark, Steven Crane, Dan Delagrange, Scott Dikkers, Thomas Greene, Matt Greiner, Jimmy Hogan, Susan M. Howard, Alicia Kraft, Alex Leviton, Andrew McNiece, Michelle Oh, Matthew Prager, Sean Smith, Ben Solomon, January Stern, Brian Sweeney, Jim Taylor, Charles Thurman, Matthew Visconage, Robert Ward

CONTRIBUTORS
Max Azulay, Megan Borgert-Spaniol, Robert Cressy, Tricia England, Kevin Horst, Doc Kane, Mel Kassel, Josh Nalven, Jenny Piette, Sean Tejaratchi, Keith Webster

DESIGNERS
Tuan Do, Kusmin, Corinne Mock, Timothy Sanders

GRAPHIC ARTISTS
Trevor Claxton, Steven Crane, Lara Demma, Charlie Dikkers, Scott Dikkers, Graham Grossman, Nataliia Letiahina, Winston McDonald, Zuyanh Nguyen, Sean Smith, Colin Strohm

COPY EDITORS
Dan Delagrange, Doc Kane

SPECIAL THANKS
Daniel Greenberg, Michael Hannus, Deborah Herman, Jeff Herman, Anton Kolyukh, *The Onion*, The Second City, Gage Skidmore, Rachel Tighe, Michael Vadon

CONTENTS

LET'S GO

A Foreword
By Donald Trump

I've written hundreds of forewords. People ask me all the time, "Donald, will you write a foreword for my book?" I'm very good at it. This is why they ask me. A lot of the forewords I've written have been for very big books. You would know the names if I told you. Big names. Much bigger than this one, I have to tell you.

How great is this foreword going to be? Let's face it, this foreword just started and it's already the best foreword you've ever read. Nobody outwrites me when it comes to forewords. Nobody.

I see bad forewords all over the place. I read a book the other day. The foreword was written by Desmond Tutu. Nice guy—I like him—but he can't write a foreword to save his life. Maybe he's a good bishop. (In fact, from what I've been told, he's a mediocre bishop.) But a foreworder? Please. He doesn't know what he's doing. I'm doing a much better job.

I've been thanked in a lot of books, too, by the way. In the acknowledgments. A lot of books. I don't think Desmond Tutu has ever been thanked in a book. I've certainly never seen it if he has.

As for this book, I'm sure it'll be a tremendous success because I wrote the foreword.

Sincerely,

Donald Trump

This Book Is Important, And Not Just Because It's About Donald Trump

An Introduction

Donald Trump is president of the United States.

In the pages ahead, you, the American citizen,* will find all the information you need to thrive under a Trump presidency. Consider this book your ultimate resource for making the most of the Trump era, which could last the next four to eight years—or more!

In this incisive guide, you'll see Donald Trump like you've never seen him before, from his earliest childhood days to his years as president and beyond. Archival photos, newspaper clippings, and other resources are presented to give you the most complete picture of what life is going to be like in Donald Trump's America, both for the entire world and for you personally. In short, it's going to be great for you. Really great (unless you are unfair to Donald Trump).

Some of the photographs and newspaper clippings in this book are from the future. How is this possible? As you will discover, in an America ruled by Donald Trump, anything is possible.

— The Editors

*If you're not an American citizen, please return this book to its rightful owner and report to a Trump Deportation Center immediately.

MEET DONALD TRUMP

THE OFFICIAL TRUMP-BRAND ORIGIN STORY

THE BIRTH OF A TRUMP

Donald Trump is proud to make public the official documentation of his birth on American soil. As president, he will display his original long-form birth certificate—a real American birth certificate for a real American—in the main foyer of the White House, framed in rich mahogany.

State of New York · County of Queens

Certificate of Birth

The New York Department of Health has filed a birth record for

Donald J. Trump ___ Date June 14, 1946

Time of birth	Midday power lunch
Hospital	Queens General Hospital penthouse suite
Skin color	Orange
Hair	Real
Eyes	Tiger
Parents' religion	Love the Bible
Parents' net worth	Over 8 million dollars
Attending physician	Some of the greatest in the world, real first-rate guys

Certified by Standard & Poor's Corp.

AAA Rating

Baby's Milestones

First Steps over Back of Poor Person
1 year 4 months

Silver Spoon

Beautiful provincial spoon hand-made by Sutter family of Cape silversmiths. Finial flourish features medallion bust of Queen Victoria, Scottish thistle, and interlocking raised flowers on matte background. Smooth bowl-front, parcel gilt upper shaft. Pleasing weight adds quality.

First Bath in Gold Coins
7 Months

So proud of our Donald. He filed civil suit against doctor who spanked him. Expect more legal action with teething.

First Lawsuit
8 weeks

Donald Trump isn't satisfied by merely releasing his official birth certificate. He's taking proof-of-birth to a new level by also releasing his baby book (excerpt above), first report card (right), an affidavit signed by his pediatrician, and an unedited, 15-year-long NBC series documenting every moment of his early childhood.

TRUMP FACT
Outraged by Eisenhower's inaction, 12-year-old Donald Trump tied all his suit jackets into long a lasso and brought down Sputnik.

Board of Education
The City of New York

REPORT CARD

P. S. 113   Borough of **Queens**
Pupil **Donald Trump**

A-Excellent   B+-Very Good   B-Good   C-Just Passable
D-Failure

Math	Incomplete - "I have a guy for that" is not an acceptable answer
Negotiation	A- (negotiated up from B)
Introduction to Yelling	A+ Donald is a natural
Bribery	A+ MY best Student!

The Brooklyn Eagle, June 22, 1952

Local Boy Suffers Undertow Accident

CONEY ISLAND

A boy was rescued after sustaining hair-related injuries Tuesday from being caught in a Coney Island undertow, local authorities reported. Donald Trump, 6, son of Queens real-estate developer Fred Trump, spent nearly 20 minutes fighting the pull of the undertow against his head before being dragged from the water.

Lifeguard Sam Stefano noticed the young Donald splashing and heroically swam out to save him, according to beach-goers on the scene. Once on the shore, he discovered the boy's hair had sustained serious damage. "I could tell right away there was something wrong with this boy's head, then I realized, 'Gosh, that is his hair.'"

The rapidly shifting hydro-dynamic forces Donald was subjected to while caught in

TRAGEDY AT SEA—Coney Island beach, above, where 6-year-old victim Donald Trump, right, was pulled under (pictured before the disfiguring hair accident).

the undertow have left his hair permanently misshapen—twisted into a wave or seashell-like form that is not recognizable as human hair.

Donald and his family were taken by ambulance to Coney Island Hospital where physicians confirmed a severe case of Traumatic Follicle Deformation. According to Staff Hair Physician Raymond Talgher,

"Patients who suffer this kind of accident will never grow normal hair again. The damage is too extensive." Dr. Talgher stated that even with corrective surgery, young Donald's hair will always be "off-putting and bizarrely malformed." He continued, "I fear we have failed little Donald, but unfortunately, medical science has only come so far."

Hospital staff reported that the boy seems to be in good spirits despite his ordeal. His family plans to leave the hospital within the next day and prepare their son for a lifetime of curious looks and whispered comments.

Said Donald's mother, Mary Trump, "Donald has always been such a kind, loving boy. I fear that, to deflect criticism of his grotesque hairdo, he will warp into an angry boy who must lash back at the world, and to overcompensate for his deformity, he will develop a dark lust for material success."

🐦 **Top Trump Tweets**

I've been fighting for America since 1951 when I punched a Korean kid in the face.

• • •

GEEKS AND NERDS TRUMP HAZED, AND HOW THEY'RE BETTER FOR IT

JIMMY VAN DUKE

Grade: 2nd

How he's better: Never looked at Trump the wrong way again.

MARY SANTINO

Grade: 1st

How she's better: Enjoys lifelong support of prescription antianxiety pills.

STEVE KRANDL

Grade: 5th

How he's better: After final, humiliating incident, never peed pants again.

ANNIE McPOWELL

Grade: 7th

How she's better: Developed eating disorder; looks great now.

Handwritten annotations:

You'll definitely make a great president of Art Club! —Brad

Dear Donald, The day you called me a 7.5 was the best day of my life xoxo Laura

I would have dated you if you had some sort of tan. —Julia Cummings

SEE YOU IN COURT —Mary Beth O'Connor

Donald, thank you for teaching me about the art of love and my financial worth. Love always, Mrs. Reynolds

Can't wait to go to Vietnam next year together! —Rob

Donald J. Trump

...ction
...-bodied
...ly 1967
...edals
...nger

Member, Sons of Young Entrepreneurs Club
Member, Under-Three-Hour Debate Club
Voted....Most Likely to Already Be Rich
....Most Likely to Write Name Very Large
...Most "Handsy"

Bern...
Vice Presiden...
Member, Drum...
Hall Moni...
Voted....Most...
....Most likel...

Toledo Blade, November 26, 1962

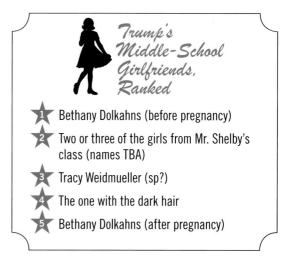

DONALD J. TRUMP, ESQ.

October 13, 1962

To Whom It Should Concern,

As one of your esteemed readers, I find the reporting in The Wharton Journal to be, frankly, lousy. In fact, it could be considered "third rate." I do not mean to be disrespectful. Actually, maybe I do. Whatever the case, this situation could potentially be a disaster.

How will students know what is happening on campus when we cannot trust the publication charged with keeping us informed? In particular, your feature "Things For Students To Do Out On The Town" was lazy reporting. Several local activities were not included on your list, such as horseback riding, enjoying a malted milk, or apple-picking.

I have to tell you, I have not written a letter calling out the shortcomings of the press since I was 9, when Highlights Magazine had to be dressed down for their reporting on tree-house construction. I felt it was unfair to tree-house developers.

Perhaps you could look for some new reporters who are smarter? The students at Brown are laughing at us when they read the - okay, I will say it - garbage that you are printing in The Wharton Journal.

I'm off to write more letters now. Maybe Playboy Magazine. Some of their centerfolds lately have not been so good.

Yours Truly,

Donald J. Trump
Sophomore

Trump's Warthogs Top Bowling Green State 14-10

PHILADELPHIA — The Wharton Warthogs football team won their second home game of the season against the BGSU Falcons Friday 14–10. Michael Sheldon paced Wharton with 109 yards on 22 carries, scoring on runs of 2 and 5 yards. Wharton's players were congratulated in the locker room after the game by their classmate and the team's owner, Donald Trump. "My guys played very well," Trump said.

STANLEY APPLEBAUM/TOLEDO BLADE STAFF

Warthogs Running Back MICHAEL SHELDON (L) carried for over 30 yards for a touchdown in the first quarter. Trump "pleased."

Long Season for Eagles

🧍‍♀️ *Trump's Middle-School Girlfriends, Ranked*

⭐1 Bethany Dolkahns (before pregnancy)

⭐2 Two or three of the girls from Mr. Shelby's class (names TBA)

⭐3 Tracy Weidmueller (sp?)

⭐4 The one with the dark hair

⭐5 Bethany Dolkahns (after pregnancy)

Starting A Business With Nothing But Elbow Grease, A Can-Do Attitude, And A Very Small Loan Of $1 Million

Many people believe Donald Trump is a self-made billionaire who forged his massive real-estate fortune out of the sweat and toil of his own bare-knuckled hands, his cowboy-like bearing in stark silhouette against the setting sun. This is correct. But before he struck it rich, Trump looked up to his father, Fred Trump, who worked tirelessly to support his family on a meager $80 million annual salary.

New York Herald Tribune, February 8, 1972

Small Real-Estate Firm Struggles to Repel Blacks Like the Big Guys

By DENNIS T. NELSON,
Staff Writer

QUEENS—Local real-estate company E. Trump & Son has been a "mom and pop" business for decades, modestly fending off Black renters in Brooklyn and Queens one family at a time. Now, with several larger property-management corporations moving into the marketplace, E. Trump & Son is beginning to feel the strain. Owner Fred Trump, 66, expressed concern for the future of his company, saying, "I've got these wonderful apartments in Coney Island. On a good day, I can keep out maybe two or three Negro families, but these big fancy conglomerates can keep out 15 or 20. How can I compete with that?"

One of the largest corporate entities in the Queens real-estate market is Consolidated Management. CEO Henry Edwards addressed their smaller competition. "Consolidated Management and these small firms are competing to deny the same service to the same unwanted customer. If we can do it better and faster, that's good for the industry, it's good for the Caucasian consumer, and it's good for the country. That's the way the free market is supposed to work."

Edwards says the failure of family companies like E. Trump & Son to keep pace, and the fact that many Black families remain in the city's apartment buildings as a result, is unfortunate, but the cost of progress.

Naturally, Fred Trump is working to prevent any slowing of Black evictions in the future. He says E. Trump & Son was founded with the simple dream of denying quality, affordable housing to Black families, and would continue to work toward that goal. One of the company's first development projects was on 198th Street in Queens building single-family houses. "I still remember the pride I felt when I told my first Negro family to take a hike. It's the moments like those that keep me in this business."

Trump says he offers something the big companies can't: fresh ideas and techniques for Black-repelling that could revolutionize the city's racially exclusive housing market. "We offer a more personal touch," he says. "My wife and I know these Negroes personally, and the fact that we can visit them in their own homes and tell them to get the hell out means so much to us."

Fred Trump plans to one day hand the business to son Donald, who is expected to begin working for the company after graduating from college. Said Donald, "The Trump family has a long-standing tradition of developing quality real estate for Whites going back to 1927, and nobody's going to take that away from us."

FRED TRUMP, who owns properties on Vernon Blvd., left, competes with large New York real-estate companies in the race to evict Blacks, and the competition puts pressure on his small business.

LOCAL, Page 18

Projects for 1972

'I'M DONALD TRUMP. WHO THE HELL ARE YOU?'

Donald Trump was a celebrity before starring on *The Apprentice* or running for president. How did he build his fame?

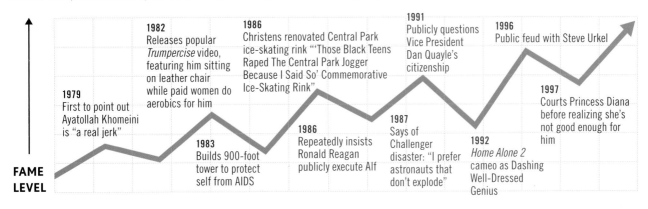

1982
Releases popular *Trumpercise* video, featuring him sitting on leather chair while paid women do aerobics for him

1986
Christens renovated Central Park ice-skating rink "'Those Black Teens Raped The Central Park Jogger Because I Said So' Commemorative Ice-Skating Rink"

1991
Publicly questions Vice President Dan Quayle's citizenship

1996
Public feud with Steve Urkel

1979
First to point out Ayatollah Khomeini is "a real jerk"

1983
Builds 900-foot tower to protect self from AIDS

1986
Repeatedly insists Ronald Reagan publicly execute Alf

1987
Says of Challenger disaster: "I prefer astronauts that don't explode"

1992
Home Alone 2 cameo as Dashing Well-Dressed Genius

1997
Courts Princess Diana before realizing she's not good enough for him

FAME LEVEL

THE VOLTRUMP INITIATIVE

Tall and majestic, Donald Trump's luxury buildings extend into the heavens. While globally renowned for their elegance and class, they're more than just magnificent properties—they're the ultimate line of defense against threats to our nation. In the event of such a threat, the buildings combine to form Voltrump.

WINNERS NEVER SLEEP

While many people would be satisfied with being a luxury real-estate mogul, multi-billionaire, top-rated television personality, multiple best-selling author, chairman and president of the Trump Organization, founder of Trump Entertainment Resorts, philanthropist, Emmy Award nominee, casino owner, university founder, world-famous billionaire investor, owner of the Miss Universe and Miss USA pageants, fine-dining restaurant owner, and president of the United States, Donald Trump is not a man to rest on his laurels. He is always creating and investing in exciting new businesses and projects.

New York Post, September 18, 2015

'Low energy' Jeb fuels Trump, Inc. drink

DONALD Trump interrupted his campaign for the Republican nomination for president Monday to introduce **Bushed**, a Trump-branded low-energy drink inspired by rival **Jeb Bush.** At a Trump Tower press conference, Trump offered the drink to not only his fellow candidate but to "anyone looking for a powerful boost of lethargy."

A jolt of Bushed promises up to one hour of push-me-down, Trump said, "for nap time, rainy weekends, when you need to lose a debate, or when you're simply looking to hit single-digit poll numbers."

Ruelers Pictures

Jeb Bush inspired Donald Trump's latest product, the low-energy drink **Bushed.**

New York Daily News, March 14, 1989

Young Casino Owner Offers Urban Kids Gambling Tips

By DEIRDRE AUERBACH

THE SIXTH GRADERS OF Brooklyn's P.S. 235 had a different kind of math class today when local real-estate developer Donald Trump visited their school to give them a special introduction to the world of gambling. Mr. Trump, who owns several casinos in Atlantic City, had been looking for a way to give back to the community. "The casino business has been very good to me, as you've probably heard, so I wanted to do something to inspire the next generation of gamblers."

Trump introduced the kids to popular table games, including roulette, craps, and blackjack, as well as various slot machines which he donated to the school. He offered tips for how much money to put into action on each game, which he said depended on how much you're winning, and wheth-

DONALD TRUMP: Giving back

er you feel lucky enough to win even more.

Trump said he hoped to leave the students with a sense of the variety and excitement that awaits them in the gaming industry. "Many children in underprivileged communities like this one have never considered a future in gambling, but I'm showing them they can win, and win big."

Trump's generosity and philanthropy had gotten through to at least some of the third graders of P.S. 235.

Twelve-year-old Jermaine Davis discovered a natural interest and enthusiasm for games of chance. "Mr. Trump taught me that math can be fun and that only morons don't split their aces." Davis and his fellow students were invited to join Trump's Junior High Roller League, a community-outreach program that offers after-school craps and poker. First to sign up was Gabriel Garcia, 11, who said, "When I grow up, I'm going to put it all on the line chasing an outside straight."

"There's a lot of potential in these kids," Trump said. "My advice to them is to double down and bet it all on a hunch."

To encourage achievement in the gambling field and recognize outstanding students, Trump has established a $2,000 high-interest loan to qualifying kids, awarded nightly.

(Deirdre Auerbach is a frequent contributor.)

Top Trump Tweets

I would have gone to Vietnam if they'd have let me shoot @JaneFonda.

BOOKS THAT AREN'T BORING

Everyone knows Donald Trump is a prolific author. He's written multiple best-selling nonfiction books on everything from business to how to be successful at business. His forays into the world of fiction have, not surprisingly, also been met with unanimous adulation. Regardless of genre, Trump's writings offer a glimpse into the mind of a one-of-a-kind American literary triumph.

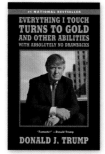

Everything I Touch Turns To Gold And Other Abilities With Absolutely No Drawbacks
(1987, Random House)
★ ★ ★ ★ ★

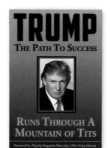

The Path To Success Runs Through A Mountain Of Tits
(1990, Random House)
★ ★ ★ ★ ★

From Riches To Riches: The Donald Trump Story
(1991, Warner Books)
★ ★ ★ ★ ★

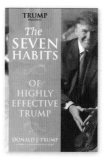

The Seven Habits Of Highly Effective Trump
(1993, Plata Publishing)
★ ★ ★ ★ ★

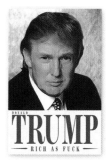

Rich As Fuck
(1996, Crown Business)
★ ★ ★ ★ ★

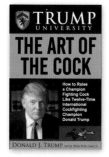

The Art Of The Cock: How To Raise A Champion Fighting Chicken
(1997, Random House)
★ ★ ★ ★ ★

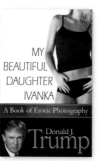

My Beautiful Daughter Ivanka: A Book Of Erotic Photography
(1999, Renaissance Books)
★ ★ ★ ★ ★

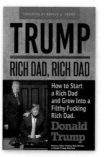

Rich Dad, Rich Dad
(2000, Times Books)
★ ★ ★ ★ ★

Mein Trumpf
(2002, Random House)
★ ★ ★ ★ ★

You're Wired! Donald Trump's Guide to Incredible Home Audio
(2004, Acapella Publishing)
★ ★ ★ ★ ★

One Nation Under Trump

(2005, Crown Business)

★ ★ ★ ★ ★

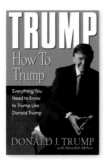

How To Trump

(2006, Crown)

★ ★ ★ ★ ★

How To Trump Like Trump

(2006, Crown Business)

★ ★ ★ ★ ★

Trumption

(2007, Random House)

★ ★ ★ ★ ★

Trump On Trump

(2007, HarperBusiness)

★ ★ ★ ★ ★

Trump Trump Trump

(2007, Warner Books)

★ ★ ★ ★ ★

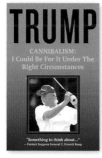

Cannibalism: I Could Be For It Under The Right Circumstances

(2009, HarperBusines)

★ ★ ★ ★ ★

An excerpt from Donald Trump's sixth and most popular volume from his Trump's Thrilling Detectives series, **Tennessee Johnny's Last Score** (1998, Vintage Crime/Black Lizard)

The fist came at Trump and he had just enough time to think it was going to hurt. He was right. Spitting the blood onto the pavement, he looked up at Darryl Crowne. "Now Crowne, use your words."

Crowne snarled and wound up for another punch. Trump hit him in his ribs. Crowne grabbed his cracked rib and let out a grunt. Trump used the opportunity to grab his hair and pull his head back. He socked Crowne right in the jaw, laying him out on his backside. He shook the blood from his nose and began to get up. The cocking of Trump's Glock 19 made him freeze in place.

"Okay, Crowne, now that that's out of your system, you're going to answer the goddamned question. Where is Victor Carlo?"

"Fuck you!"

Trump sighed, then pressed the heel of his wing-tip into Crowne's cracked rib, releasing a howl.

"Would you like to rethink your answer?"

"Okay, okay!" Crowne cried out. Trump took his foot off the rib. Crowne caught his breath. "The last I heard, Vic was going over to Mikey's."

"Who the hell is Mikey? Mikey Bivona?"

"No man, Mikey's, the titty bar on 14th and Western."

"They got good wings there."

"Yeah." Crowne inhaled. "So, are we fucking done here?"

"Yeah, we're done."

Trump slugged Crowne in the jaw one last time just for kicks, then walked to his Lincoln Town Car, leaving Crowne on the ground. As he drove away, he shifted in his seat uncomfortably. The last time he was at Mikey's, the owner told him that if he ever showed his face in there again he would personally blow it off with the sawed-off he kept under the bar.

I Am Trump
(2008, Wiley)
★★★★★

Trump: Trump
(2009, Crown Business)
★★★★★

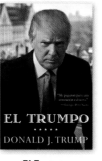

El Trumpo
(2009, Times Books)
★★★★★

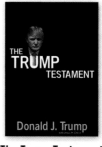

The Trump Testament
(2011, Regnery Publishing)
★★★★★

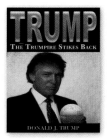

The Trumpire Strikes Back
(2013, Vanguard Press)
★★★★★

The Only Three Emotions You Need And How To Use Them
(2013, Crown Business)
★★★★★

The Art Of Dealing With The Loss Of A Pet Bird
(2015, Simon and Schuster)
★★★★★

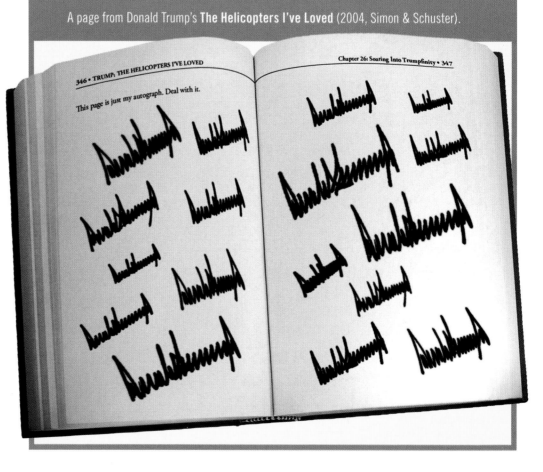

A page from Donald Trump's **The Helicopters I've Loved** (2004, Simon & Schuster).

346 • TRUMP: THE HELICOPTERS I'VE LOVED

Chapter 26: Soaring Into Trumpfinity • 347

This page is just my autograph. Deal with it.

New York Post, July 28, 2011

Donald Trump wins again outside the Blimpie on 3rd Ave in Manhattan

Grace

Gale Lynch/UPI

Trump card wins free sandwich

Three days after dropping his business card into a plastic jar at the **Blimpie** on 3rd Avenue, billionaire businessman **Donald Trump** received word Friday he'd won a free sandwich from the sub shop.

"You might think my odds were slim when I put my card in that big jar with, like, a hundred others," the wealthy businessman said upon receiving the news. "But this is what I do. I win." Trump left his office immediately to claim the prize, telling associates, "This is perfect. I knew I would win, and I knew this is what I would have for lunch today."

At Blimpie, Trump is said to have ordered the deli tuna sandwich with no lettuce before asking the Blimpie employee whether his prize came with a combo fountain drink and cookie. According to clerks, the business executive and reality-TV personality was visibly upset upon learning extras were not included, but perked up considerably when told he was still eligible to enter his card in the next drawing. "I will get what I am entitled to from Blimpie," Trump said.

TRUMP FACT
Everyone fired on *The Apprentice* was donated to charity.

A COUNTRY PLEADS

Pundits and politicos had long anticipated Donald Trump would one day run for president. These rarely seen campaign buttons mark Trump's extraordinary journey not listening to those people.

1988 — TRUMP "IT IS SOMETHING I WOULD CONSIDER" 1988

1992 — MAYBE '92 '92 NEXT TIME

1996 — IT COULD HAPPEN BUT PROBABLY NOT

2000 — DONALD TRUMP 2000 IT'S A POSSIBILITY

2004 — TRUMP '04 eh

2008 — THE DONALD 2008 MAYBE

2012 — TRUMP Really, maybe

2016 — OK "You Finally Deserve Me"

PRESIDENT TRUMP

AMERICA'S NEW BOSS

PUTTING THE "EXECUTIVE" IN "EXECUTIVE BRANCH"

The world changed on the afternoon of Friday, January 20, 2017, a day that will forever be remembered as the day America became great again. Donald J. Trump stood in front of millions of adoring citizens and was formally sworn in as the 45th president of the United States. Men, women, and children alike wept at the greatness bestowed upon us.

TRUMP
INTERNATIONAL HOTEL & TOWER
NEW YORK

Inaugural Address by Donald J. Trump (ROUGH DRAFT)

Thank you, Chief Justice (???????) ...I want to thank the good people who voted for me. Fantastic job. You nailed it. You treated me very well. To be honest, it was an easy decision, but still, good for you.

The rest of you... Should I say it? Should I? Ok, I'll say it. You let us all down. What can I tell you?

(wait for Applause to die down) I'm honored to stand here today as your 45th president, stepping into the role that so many great men have filled. Well... they're not all great. Don't get me wrong, some of them were good. But frankly most of them are overrated. I won't get into details now, but a few were real losers.

But today isn't about the mistakes of the past. It's about me being President. Honestly, that's why we're here, isn't it? (Big applause here)

This Nation has seen better days. America is not a big money-maker. I don't need the money from this job, by the way, I can tell you that, it's not a big deal. (ad lib how rich). Our country needs to start being smarter, making better deals. Iran is walking all over us. Mexico is eating our lunch. And China.

Beginning now we're going to be winning. A lot. You've got good leadership now, so that's a good start. I'll turn this whole thing around so fast, it'll make your head spin. We're going to make America great again. Big league.

Thank you. You've been a wonderful crowd. Not the biggest crowd I've ever spoken to, but pretty big. Thank you.

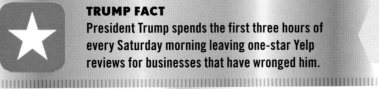

TRUMP FACT
President Trump spends the first three hours of every Saturday morning leaving one-star Yelp reviews for businesses that have wronged him.

Donald Trump swears to uphold the dignity of the office of president of the United States.

Top Trump Tweets

I'm refusing the pathetic presidential salary. Will donate every penny to breast enhancement research. #charity

...

TO BE THROWN OUT OF THE WHITE HOUSE ON DAY ONE

1. Any administrative assistant over 26
2. Any lighting that doesn't set a mood
3. Sasha's hermit crab
4. Traditional "Letter to My Successor" from Obama
5. Photos or paintings of Obama family, except Michelle
6. Any leftover chitlins
7. Hideous fixtures
8. Red phone (to be replaced with gold phone)

9. Obama's Koran
10. Any wall that isn't mirrored
11. All doors that don't confer respect
12. China
13. Anything under $100,000 in value
14. Tiny 60-inch TVs
15. Lincoln's ghost
16. Roger Clinton
17. Congress
18. Supreme Court
19. Mail from chumps

20. Anything wooden or silver that could be driven into Trump's heart
21. Hispanic sous chef
22. Magical orb containing what's left of the American dream
23. The hoodlum-attracting basketball court
24. Muslim-y rugs
25. Grimley, the White House special-needs chimney sweep
26. Cheap-ass Marine One helicopter

OUR NEW FIRST FAMILY

The Mighty Seed Of Trump

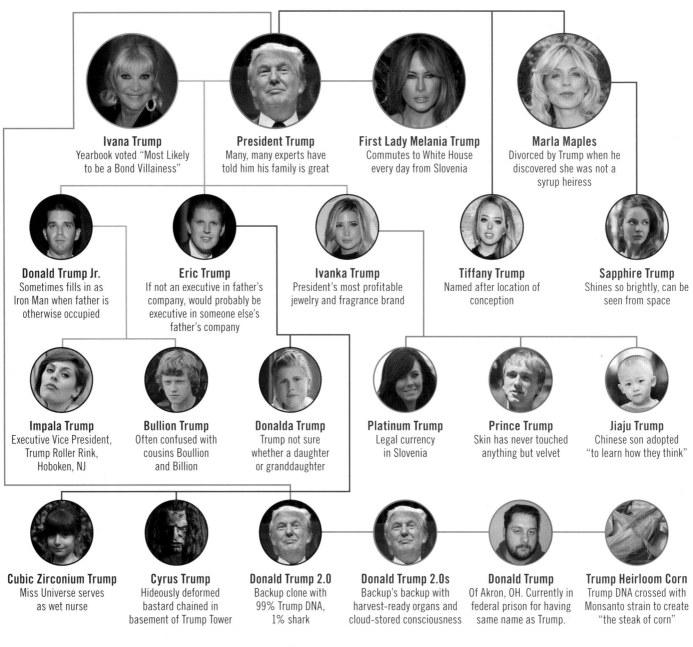

Ivana Trump
Yearbook voted "Most Likely to be a Bond Villainess"

President Trump
Many, many experts have told him his family is great

First Lady Melania Trump
Commutes to White House every day from Slovenia

Marla Maples
Divorced by Trump when he discovered she was not a syrup heiress

Donald Trump Jr.
Sometimes fills in as Iron Man when father is otherwise occupied

Eric Trump
If not an executive in father's company, would probably be executive in someone else's father's company

Ivanka Trump
President's most profitable jewelry and fragrance brand

Tiffany Trump
Named after location of conception

Sapphire Trump
Shines so brightly, can be seen from space

Impala Trump
Executive Vice President, Trump Roller Rink, Hoboken, NJ

Bullion Trump
Often confused with cousins Boullion and Billion

Donalda Trump
Trump not sure whether a daughter or granddaughter

Platinum Trump
Legal currency in Slovenia

Prince Trump
Skin has never touched anything but velvet

Jiaju Trump
Chinese son adopted "to learn how they think"

Cubic Zirconium Trump
Miss Universe serves as wet nurse

Cyrus Trump
Hideously deformed bastard chained in basement of Trump Tower

Donald Trump 2.0
Backup clone with 99% Trump DNA, 1% shark

Donald Trump 2.0s
Backup's backup with harvest-ready organs and cloud-stored consciousness

Donald Trump
Of Akron, OH. Currently in federal prison for having same name as Trump.

Trump Heirloom Corn
Trump DNA crossed with Monsanto strain to create "the steak of corn"

DONALD TRUMP'S CHILDREN: RANKED BY TRUMP

1. IVANKA TRUMP

"Successful, bright, and the best body you've ever seen."

2. DONALD TRUMP JR.

"A terrific name."

3. ERIC TRUMP

"Good kid. A man's man and a killer. Hunts baby cheetahs."

4. THE REST

"Look, they're all great. One thing I will say is that I wish more of them had Wikipedia pages so I could keep up with what they're doing."

THINGS YOU'LL NEED IN TRUMP'S AMERICA

Whatever the opposite of a Spanish dictionary is

★

Personal hand-written apology letter to Trump for making America bad

★

Statement of your net worth

★

Your own damn ideas for making America great again

★

Extra-absorbent kerchiefs from the Ivanka Trump Signature Collection

SUPERMAN, CAN YOU HEAR ME!? SUPERMAN, WHERE ARE YOU!?

MEET THE "FIRST" LADY
Melania Trump

As is customary, the First Lady will champion a cause close to her heart: closing her eyes and pretending she's not having sex with Donald Trump.

Slovenian-born model and jewelry designer Melania Trump brings effortless grace and elegance to the White House. She will use her position to promote awareness of her signature issue. "Closing my eyes and pretending I'm not having sex with Donald Trump is the most important mission in my life," Mrs. Trump says, "and I will give this issue the national attention it deserves." She'll launch the "Just Think No" campaign, and speak to schoolchildren across the nation about her hope to escape into a "world of the mind" far, far away during sex with her husband. She believes her message will inspire young people to understand the importance of gritting her teeth and somehow suffering through yet another abhorrent bout of Donald Trump-initiated intercourse. "If we Americans can send a man to the moon," she says, "then surely I can block out the sound of this repugnant man grunting his own name over and over while he penetrates me."

FIRST LADY FACTS

- Genuinely likes "the people"
- Enjoys long walks on the beach that her husband installed on the 35th floor of Trump Tower
- Passionate about saving endangered minks
- Unaware marriage has term limit

TRUMP FACT

Every Valentine's Day, Donald Trump gives his wife a single, chocolate-covered baboon heart.

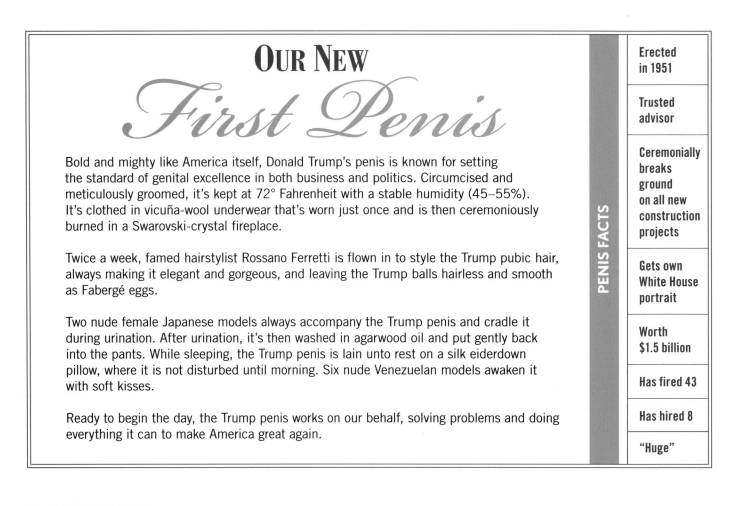

OUR NEW
First Penis

Bold and mighty like America itself, Donald Trump's penis is known for setting the standard of genital excellence in both business and politics. Circumcised and meticulously groomed, it's kept at 72° Fahrenheit with a stable humidity (45–55%). It's clothed in vicuña-wool underwear that's worn just once and is then ceremoniously burned in a Swarovski-crystal fireplace.

Twice a week, famed hairstylist Rossano Ferretti is flown in to style the Trump pubic hair, always making it elegant and gorgeous, and leaving the Trump balls hairless and smooth as Fabergé eggs.

Two nude female Japanese models always accompany the Trump penis and cradle it during urination. After urination, it's then washed in agarwood oil and put gently back into the pants. While sleeping, the Trump penis is lain unto rest on a silk eiderdown pillow, where it is not disturbed until morning. Six nude Venezuelan models awaken it with soft kisses.

Ready to begin the day, the Trump penis works on our behalf, solving problems and doing everything it can to make America great again.

PENIS FACTS

Erected in 1951
Trusted advisor
Ceremonially breaks ground on all new construction projects
Gets own White House portrait
Worth $1.5 billion
Has fired 43
Has hired 8
"Huge"

New York Post, May 12, 2017

Majority of Trump Wikipedia edits traced to Oval Office

WASHINGTON — The majority of edits to the Wikipedia page of President Donald Trump have been traced to an IP address in the Oval Office, sources confirmed Monday. Over 70 percent of 7,531 edits over the past six months were made by the user WikiWinner. Wikipedia officials confirmed that details updated from the Oval Office IP address included a new section on "Trump's real hair," a repeated lowering of his age, and the addition of a claim that Trump is the first president whose "sex number" is greater than 500. Although the identity of WikiWinner could not be established, Wikipedia has suspended the user's access. The White House has not responded to the findings except to issue a brief statement of intent to "shut down" Wikipedia.

THE FIRESIDE SCOLDINGS
A New American Tradition

One of the cherished hallmarks of Donald Trump's presidency is surely his weekly fireside scoldings. Just as FDR's famous fireside chats soothed a nation in the grip of the Great Depression and World War II, Trump's fireside scoldings repudiate a nation full of morons, lightweights, and clowns.

NOTABLE FIRESIDE SCOLDINGS

JANUARY 22, 2017

Dressing Down, Individually And By Name, Everyone Who Didn't Vote For Trump

JUNE 11, 2017

Police And Blacks, Knock It Off— Race War Solved

NOVEMBER 18, 2018

@Jeremy0298, I Saw What You Said On Twitter

MAY 5, 2019

The Restaurants In Trump Hotels Spend Thousands Annually On After-Dinner Mints That Nobody Eats

SEPTEMBER 27, 2020

Hawaiians, Your Pizza Is A Disgrace

APRIL 24, 2022

You Should Be Thanking Me

DECEMBER 4, 2022

Florida's Orange Growers: Terrible At Their Jobs And Worse Than ISIS

JUNE 18, 2023

The Tattletales Who Ruin A Steamy Student-Teacher Relationship

DECEMBER 31, 2023

Nobody's Leaving This Room Until I Find Out Who Wrote "President Chump" In The Oval Office Guestbook

MARCH 17, 2024

The Time You Sent An Email And Forgot To CC Me

An excerpt from July 4, 2020: Americans Are Stupid

"You people are stupid—not all of you. Some of you may be smart. But I get letters—a lot of letters. I don't read them. I have people who read them. And sometimes they'll show me a letter. And I can't believe what I'm seeing. You people can't write. You can't spell. What are you even saying? 'I can't afford college, Trump. Please help me. Blah blah blah.' You're too stupid to go to college. Go to a barbecue."

33

Say Hello To The New First Pet

The official pet of Donald Trump's White House is Strongy, an 800-pound silverback gorilla. Americans enjoy watching the loyal pet chase down and flip over the vice president's motorcade, play fetch with the nuclear football, or come out of nowhere to mount visiting foreign dignitaries. Rest assured, everyone who meets Strongy will fall in love with his never-scripted and always straight-from-the-heart feces throwing and public masturbating.

FIRST PET FACTS

Housebroken: No

Trained To Ignore Any Commands Given By A Woman: Yes

The First Presidential Pet To Kill A Man: Yes

Can Deliver Bills From Congress Without Eating Them: No

FIRST PET'S RESPONSIBILITIES

It isn't all fun and games for Strongy. He has some important duties as the nation's First Pet.

★ Testing President Trump's food before he eats it

★ Body double for the president at boring meetings

★ Sign language translator when the president insults the deaf

★ 12th in line for the presidency

Top Trump Tweets

@Melania is a tremendous First Lady. When do I get to pick the Second Lady?

• • •

TRUMP FACT
In the Trump White House, interns are subject to surprise massages.

15 WAYS THE STATE OF THE UNION ADDRESS CAN TURN A PROFIT

Many of the constitutionally mandated practices of our democracy have been operating at a financial loss for more than 200 years. President Trump won't stand for that. A smart businessman doesn't leave money on the table. Here are just a few ways he can leverage one of our countless forgotten, long-dead government assets: the State of the Union address.

1. $100 a head ($200 if not born in U.S.)
2. Pay-per-view
3. Product placement
4. Concessions
5. Merchandise
6. Multi-city tour
7. Partner with Expedia to sell vacation packages for honored guests
8. Rousey vs. Holm undercard
9. Sell naming rights
10. Unrated version
11. State of the Union: The Game
12. Gold-level package subscribers get real State of the Union address
13. Crossover with Marvel
14. Sue past presidents for use of Trump Organization trademarked phrase, "My Fellow Americans"
15. Christmas version

The New York Times, January 9, 2018

Trump Rebuts Every Negative Response to State of the Union

By MARK FLEMMNG and JANICE WEISMAN

WASHINGTON—President Donald Trump concluded his State of the Union address Tuesday night by vowing to rebut each and every negative response, starting with the official Democratic response, but not stopping there.

"Every American deserves to be given a simple 'You're wrong and I'm right,'" Trump said at the close of his 90-minute improvised speech to Congress.

The president spent the next few hours returning volley after volley of YouTube comments, tweets, and blog postings addressing any critic who gave his speech less than effusive praise.

Sources confirmed early this morning the bleary-eyed president struggled to stay focused during his daily intelligence briefing as he thumbed through more than 200 lukewarm responses to his speech on Facebook, which he promised to immediately fact-check or dismiss with a derogatory insult.

At press time, the president was said to have canceled today's meeting with Israeli Prime Minister Benjamin Netanyahu to stay on top of any slights made by the nation's morning-radio DJs.

Continued on Page A13

STUPID WHITE HOUSE TRADITIONS THAT WILL BE BANISHED

To the great relief of the American people, President Trump will discontinue several White House and presidential traditions. "These traditions are stupid and a waste of my time," President Trump says. He will banish these "pathetic" activities and replace them with "fantastic, better ones," which will in turn become the cherished traditions of future presidents.

OLD TRADITION	NEW TRADITION
Pardoning the Thanksgiving turkey	President Trump will take the honorary first bite of the turkey's deep-fried gizzard.
Hosting championship sports teams	President Trump will host Tom Brady after every major sports championship.
White House Easter egg hunt for children	The president will find the most eggs and defeat every child who joins in the Easter egg hunt.
Giving away pens after bill signing	These are good pens. If people want one, they will be charged $5,000 per pen.
Reading "'Twas the Night Before Christmas" to children at Christmas	The president will read *Crippled America* to children at Christmas.
Outgoing president leaving a note for the incoming president	The outgoing president will leave an autographed 8"x10" photo of Trump for the incoming president.

Roller Coasters, Sandals, Corn Dogs, and Watches: Trump On The Issues

ROLLER COASTERS

"They're great, but why are they so short? If I were running the theme park, all the rides would be 30 minutes long, minimum. And they need better leaders. The people who put you in the roller coaster and put the safety bar down—they're clowns. Have you been to Six Flags? Great park, terrific rides. But the people who work there are some of the biggest losers you've ever seen—and I've seen a lot. Bottom line: roller coasters need to be longer. Period."

SANDALS

"These are a no-brainer. People buy half a shoe for the price of a full shoe. It's smart business. I don't wear them because they're disgusting and they make you look dumb. And I wouldn't sell them because they don't fit the Trump brand. However, if I did sell them, they would make me a lot of money. Do you know how much it costs to make a sandal in China or one of the other countries? I do. I called one of the best shoe men, a good friend

of mine. He told me. If you knew the price, you wouldn't have to ask. That's your first lesson. Write it down."

CORN DOGS

"Think of it. How much money do you save by not having to buy the bun? I'll have to ask some people I know, but I'm guessing it's a lot. And a lot of people will pay a premium for it. But not me. I don't eat food on a stick."

WATCHES

"Who wears watches to tell time? People with no class. I wear a watch, but not to tell time. I wear it as jewelry. It's a very nice watch. If I need to know what time it is, my people tell me. Chinese watches are very poorly made. The Japanese make a good watch, but I don't trust them. They've got robots. Watch the news. You'll see. Ask any watchmaker about wearing a watch if you don't believe me. I know some very smart watchmakers. They're Jewish and I guarantee they know more about watches than the Chinese."

DONALD TRUMP'S PRESIDENTIAL SCHEDULE

Presidential routines are as varied as the officeholders themselves. Regular habits speak volumes about the tone and character of a presidency. What may seem like insignificant, day-to-day pursuits of the commander in chief are ultimately what shape his legacy. Here is an intimate look at a typical day in the Trump White House.

TRUMP FACT
President Trump is spending $20 million to renovate his emergency bunker so it looks amazing when he broadcasts from it.

6:00 AM	President sits down in study with leading newspapers to read all the articles about himself
7:00 AM	Over breakfast with First Family, orders FBI surveillance on select reporters
7:30 AM	Colors in segment on giant posterboard thermometer to indicate how close we are to officially making America great again
9:35 AM	Photo-op with Chinese Ambassador
9:45 AM	Chinese debt crisis solved
12:15 PM	Lunch meeting with Secretary of Education and cast of new Avengers movie
12:30 PM	Private meeting with Mark Ruffalo to berate terrible performance in new Avengers movie
1:00 PM	Visits Ford Motor Company assembly plant (hard hat required)
1:05 PM	Emergency 2-hour session with stylist to address "hat hair"
2:00 PM	Meeting with Congressional Black Caucus - CANCELLED INDEFINITELY due to stylist appointment running over
4:30 PM	President reviews day's events with personal secretary and updates Presidential Enemies list
8:05 PM	Private meeting with stepson to explain Grays Sports Almanac
9:25 PM	President and First Lady retire to the residence
9:45 PM	President informs Secret Service detail: "I just banged my hot model wife"
9:46 PM	Secret Service agent complies with order to give President a high five

THE GREAT TRUMP SPEECHES WE'LL REMEMBER FOR GENERATIONS

"MY HAIR IS REAL"

February 23, 2017, New York, NY
Address to the United Nations General Assembly
"People think my hair is fake or that I wear a toupee. That's ridiculous! Anyone from any country, come and pull my hair. China? Italy? Come on. Pull it. I'll tell you exactly where to pull it and how, once you're up here. Let's go. Come on up."

"MR. NO-GOOD HOOLIGAN, CLEAN UP THIS WALL"

August 12, 2018, the Texas-Arizona border
Speech to border guards and local officials
"Mr. Unknown Vandal, you're not going to get away with this. I promise you that. Find a big brush. Get a bucket and some soap, because Mr. Worthless Piece of Garbage who drew the 90-mile-long penis along the U.S.-Mexico border, clean up this wall!"

THE NEW HOTEL BUILT OVER THE GETTYSBURG CEMETERY ADDRESS

November 19, 2020, Gettysburg, PA
Address to builders and developers of the Gettysburg Chamber of Commerce
"Four score and I don't know how many years ago—lot of years—Abraham Lincoln gave a great speech about this place. A good speech, we'll say. An okay speech. But we're here today to break ground on a really nice piece of property. A great hotel. The parking lot will go right here. It is altogether fitting and proper that we should do this."

"ASK NOT WHAT YOUR COUNTRY CAN DO FOR YOU, ASK WHAT YOU CAN BUY FROM THE TRUMP COLLECTION GIFT STORE"

January 21, 2021, Washington, DC
Second inaugural address
"There are so many great deals in the Trump Collection gift store right now. These are great for Valentine's Day, which is coming up. If you really want to give the gift of class, or give the gift that will tell your loved ones that you really care, and that you think of them as worth an expensive luxury item, and that you have that kind of disposable income—very important—we've got it. Chandeliers, satin bedding, nice socks even. It's all wonderful stuff."

"I HAVE A PLANE"

August 28, 2023, Washington, DC
Speech to assembled marchers on the Washington Mall
"I have a plane. I have a plane that will one day rise up over this nation and live out the true meaning of the words, 'luxury air travel.' I have a plane."

HOW DOES PRESIDENT TRUMP COPE WITH LIVING IN A PLAIN WHITE HOUSE BUILT FOR POOR MEN?

Built in 1792, the White House may have seemed like suitable quarters at the time, but that was also a time when man could only move as fast as a horse could run. A lot has changed since then! The nation will no longer tolerate its president traveling by horse, and nor should it now tolerate its first family being relegated to a rickety, 200-year-old, colorless hovel that's scarcely bigger than 50,000 square feet. After the sacrifices they've made on the campaign trail, they deserve better.

The president's new home, Trump Presidential Plaza, will feature over 200,000 square feet of premium retail space in addition to 116 luxury condominiums, a state-of-the-art office complex where the president will work, and a 10-story executive penthouse where the first family can finally live and grow in peace, far from the intrusion of tour groups or the press. The original White House will be preserved as a historical attraction within the plaza, part of an interior courtyard surrounded by a five-star food court and amusement-park-style rides, including the world's tallest marble waterslide.

Upon the complex's grand opening in June 2018, Americans can finally take pride in the residence of their commander in chief, a house of grandeur befitting the greatest leader of the world's greatest nation. Visitors from all over the world who pass the religious test will be welcomed through its grand south entrance, marked by a towering row of letters that will include the renovated Washington Monument serving as the vertical segment of the "T" in "TRUMP," at the apex of which will be a rotating five-star restaurant and casino.

MEMO TO WHITE HOUSE STAFF: HOW TO UNSEE WHAT YOU'VE JUST SEEN

As the White House domestic staff begins serving a new administration, they must also adjust to living with a new family who calls the official residence their home. This internal memo provides an intimate look at how White House attendants, housekeeping, and other staff will maintain their tact and aplomb as they organize, sanitize, and beautify 1600 Pennsylvania Avenue.

M E M O R A N D U M

Date: February 21, 2017

To: White House Residence Staff

From: Margaret Hagestad, White House Chief Usher

RE: How to Unsee What You've Just Seen

There may be a time when you see something you immediately wish you had not seen. In these moments, you must exercise extreme discretion. Do not acknowledge to the President or First Family what you have seen. Instead, retreat and remove the incident from your mind's eye forever.

Blocking out what you've seen may be difficult under certain circumstances. I recommend the following:

- Any strange stains found on the President's laundry are likely from a type of béarnaise sauce you've never encountered before.
- Beautiful, exotic women roaming the halls are the responsibility of the Secret Service. Ignore them.
- Any maps or globes with large red X's over many countries were like that before Trump bought them. Dust and move on.
- When working near the President's large meditation pod, if you glimpse what you believe to be splotchy red spots or scars on the back of his anemic scalp as something orange is mechanically lowered onto his head, be advised that this is simply a grooming routine involving his natural hair and certain creams.
- The President hosts many lavish events with many influential people. The figures you may have seen sharing cigars with the President were part of an extraterrestrial-themed party.
- The vacuum-sealed steel door marked "Gene Replication Facility" is nothing more than a donated prop from one of the President's film-industry friends.

Contact me if you have questions or require immediate counseling.

APPLAUSE

1. Luxury booths for visiting NFL owners

2. White grand piano with blind pianist

3. On hot days, spritzers spray cool mist of Trump Ice spring water

4. Presidential seal on podium slides open to reveal even larger presidential seal

5. All questions must be asked in the form of genuflection

6. Emergency medical zone in case female reporter has to deal with what's going on "down there"

7. Remote-control electric shockers under seats

8. Bouncers

9. Ticket-taker

10. Caddy

11. Roulette wheel

12. Framed magazine covers featuring President Trump

13. All journalists checked for Hispanicness at entrance

14. When President Trump tires of answering questions, podium is blocked by raised flat-screen which displays real-time feed of president's tweets

15. Applause sign

16. Standard reporter seating ($): admittance to Q&A, but not allowed to ask questions

17. Premium reporter seating ($$): admittance to Q&A plus gift bag

18. Platinum reporter seating ($$$): admittance to Q&A, gift bag, plus picture with President Trump

19. Animatronic reporters who stand up and ask flattering questions

20. Stockade

21. Small crawl space on dirt path where disgraced reporters can exit like dogs

22. Booby-trap door

23. "Speaking Scepter": solid-gold scepter featuring bust of Trump. (Only those holding Speaking Scepter may speak.)

24. Ticker showing up-to-the-minute updates of President Trump's personal net worth

25. Button that plays "We're Not Gonna Take It" over annoying questions

26. Section for hot weather girls

27. Podium converts into escape rocket

28. Breast-feeding shame room

29. Slot machines and all-you-can-eat shrimp buffet laced with Ambien

30. Giant aquarium with mermaids

31. White House fact-checkers at door to approve every reporter notebook

32. Reporter-delousing chamber

33. Emergency Zyklon-B gas dispenser

THE NEW, IMPROVED WHITE HOUSE PRESSROOM

The old White House Pressroom was as plain and boring as its uninspiring name. Little more than a room with a podium, this sad excuse for a presidential platform failed to project the grandeur and stately tone you can expect when a truly great president addresses the dishonest jackasses in the media.

TRUMP'S GUIDE TO JOURNALISTIC INTEGRITY

FACT-CHECKING
If President Trump says it out loud and tweets it, consider that two sources confirming the information.

OBJECTIVITY
Objectively praising President Trump's many strengths is a sign of great credibility.

PUBLISHING CORRECTIONS
To ensure the people of the world get only accurate information from newspapers, President Trump alerts reporters of specific errors by mailing their articles back to them strewn with handwritten insults.

PUBLIC INTEREST VS. PRIVACY
The public has great interest in President Trump, so request a private audience with him and he will tell you what you should write.

ANONYMOUS SOURCES
If a source cannot be directly attacked on Twitter, it should never be included in your reporting.

PLAGIARISM
If you have any doubt a smart or insightful phrase is originally yours, be safe and assume you are plagiarizing a passage from *The Art of the Deal.*

CONFLICT OF INTEREST
Any party in conflict with President Trump must be discredited with interesting quotes from President Trump.

BYLINES
All articles about President Trump should credit him as a writer, since he provided the key source material. The appropriate royalty must follow as negotiated.

RELATIONSHIPS WITH SOURCES
A source must not be revealed unless it is a beautiful source, in which case President Trump must not be denied the pleasure.

THANK YOU LETTER
Mentioning Donald Trump in your writing will make it successful. Be sure to take the time to write him a thank you note, and follow up by praising him on Twitter.

TRUMP FACT
Trump replaced all synthetic fixtures in the White House with genuine free-range ivory.

PRESIDENT TRUMP: AMERICA'S NEW BOSS

INSTRUCTIONS FOR PHOTOGRAPHERS
HOW TO TAKE THE BEST PHOTOS OF TRUMP

 To accentuate Trump's youthful features, photographs are best taken between 1964 and 1985.

 Camera must angle up 45 degrees to convey deference.

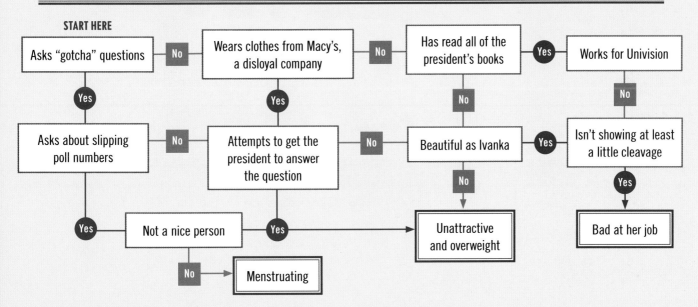 In some photos, Trump may appear with red, demonic eyes. Unfortunately, there is no way to correct this.

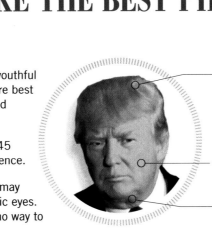

If winds are NNE at more than 3 mph, all camera equipment must face due west to ensure proper hair position.

To give skin healthy glow, lighting must only come from gold or crystal chandelier.

Photo retouching is unethical in journalism, unless it's to highlight the true radiance of Trump's turkey neck.

> Top Trump Tweets
>
> I'll defund Planned Parenthood and use the $$ for something the USA really needs: more active duty Ghostbusters.

★ ★ ★ HOW TO TELL IF A REPORTER IS BAD AT HER JOB ★ ★ ★

START HERE

Asks "gotcha" questions — **No** → Wears clothes from Macy's, a disloyal company — **No** → Has read all of the president's books — **Yes** → Works for Univision

Asks "gotcha" questions — **Yes** ↓

Asks about slipping poll numbers — **No** → Attempts to get the president to answer the question — **No** → Beautiful as Ivanka — **Yes** → Isn't showing at least a little cleavage

Wears clothes from Macy's, a disloyal company — **Yes** ↓ Attempts to get the president to answer the question

Has read all of the president's books — **No** ↓ Beautiful as Ivanka

Works for Univision — **No** ↓ Isn't showing at least a little cleavage

Asks about slipping poll numbers — **Yes** ↓ Not a nice person — **Yes** → Unattractive and overweight

Attempts to get the president to answer the question — **Yes** → Unattractive and overweight

Beautiful as Ivanka — **No** ↓ Unattractive and overweight

Isn't showing at least a little cleavage — **Yes** ↓ Bad at her job

Not a nice person — **No** → Menstruating

HARD LINE: Prez won't return calls from 'amateur' deal makers from ISIS

US 'won't negotiate with terrorists unless they bring A-game'

By CARMINE PURVIS

WASHINGTON — President Trump clarified his position on terrorist negotiations at a White House press conference today, stating his refusal to engage in discussions unless ISIS officials "really bring it." Trump pledged to walk away from any "hack" terrorist-negotiators: "When they come to the table dressed in dirty rags, that's not treating me with any respect. If they would come in a suit and tie with nice dress shoes, then I know I'm dealing with serious people." Trump expressed a lack of faith that negotiations with ISIS will be successful. "We could have a good deal; a win-win deal. But these people so far are not very impressive. They undercut their value and don't even know a dollar figure for their cut-and-run point. Basic stuff, folks." Trump told reporters he has sent top ISIS commanders several Arabic translations of "The Art of the Deal" and is waiting for their rave reviews.

The Presidential Ring, a revered emblem of our government's executive branch, was bestowed on President Donald Trump during the four-hour Ringing Ceremony on Ring Day, January 30, 2017

Weight: 6 pounds

★

Designer: Tiffany's, in cooperation with Tiffany Trump

★

Center: Grade-S tinted diamond carved in replica of Trump International Hotel and Tower, New York. 1.2 inches square and gold-gilded. "TRUMP" set in hand-set 4Cs stones along the rim.

Top: Embossed presidential-seal stamp with interchangeable heated-wax tip and cabinet-member branding iron

★

Band: Handpicked IF-rated 75-point diamonds in shape of Trump's Turnberry, Scotland, golf course. Sand pits rendered as golden divots.

Trump's Presidential Ring

Special Features

Emits spray of Success By Trump® cologne on the half hour
Acts as a precious-metal detector calibrated to 0.4mm-metal-sphere accuracy
Flip-out screen shows surveillance video from Trump Tower entrance
Siri
Hums when precious metals are present
Functions as golf tee rated for tournament play

```
                                        UNITED STATES GOVERNMENT
                                          M E M O R A N D U M
                                         U.S. SECRET SERVICE
```

FROM: OFFICE OF THE DIRECTOR

DATE: NOV. 9, 2016   10:01 AM

SUBJECT: SPECIAL DETAIL FOR NEW POTUS

TO: ALL AGENTS

POTUS HAS ORDERED NEW TOP-SECRET DETACHMENT OF SECRET SERVICE.

IN ACCORDANCE WITH DIRECT POTUS ORDER, DETACHMENT DETAIL: TWO (2)
AGENTS ASSIGNED TO ACCOMPANY POTUS AT CLOSE DISTANCE TO PROVIDE
SECURITY AND MAINTAIN INTEGRITY OF POTUS ███.

UNIT DIRECTED BY POTUS WILL BE RESPONSIBLE FOR PROTECTING POTUS
████ (ON HEAD, NECK, AND UPPER FACE) FROM BEING EXPOSED AS A ████
████ TO THE PUBLIC OF THE UNITED STATES AND THE WORLD.

POTUS ████ WILL BE REFERRED TO BY CODE NAME: "EAGLE'S NEST"

ADDITIONAL DUTY: AGENTS WILL PROVIDE COVER AND PROTECTION TO ████
CLUB FOR MEN PERSONNEL WHO WILL MEET WITH POTUS FROM TIME TO TIME
TO ASSESS, CALIBRATE, AND/OR CLEAN EAGLE'S NEST.

EMERGENCY PROTOCOL: IN THE EVENT OF LOSS OF STABILITY, INTEGRITY,
AND/OR CONTAINMENT OF EAGLE'S NEST, AGENTS WILL SHIELD EAGLE'S
NEST FROM PUBLIC VIEW BY WAY OF: UMBRELLA, HAT, THEIR OWN BODIES.
NO LOSS OF CONTAINMENT RE: EAGLE'S NEST ALLOWED. AGENTS WILL
CARRY CASE CONTAINING TEMPORARY ████████ (HEREBY KNOWN AS
"BACKUP EAGLE'S NEST") IN INSTANCES OF EXTREME WEATHER (RAIN,
HIGH WINDS, OTHER CONDITION HAZARDOUS TO EAGLE'S NEST.)

POTUS ORDERS: AGENTS WILL NOT DEVIATE FROM SAID DUTY. WILL
PROVIDE DISCREET 24 HR COVERAGE WITHIN LESS THAN 10 FEET FROM
POTUS FACE AND HEAD AT ALL TIMES. WILL NOT BE ASSIGNED TO OTHER
DETAIL. WILL NOT TAKE ACTIVE ROLE IN PROTECTION OF POTUS PER SE,
ONLY EAGLE'S NEST. WILL NOT AID POTUS EVEN IN MEDICAL CODE ALPHA.
SOLE FOCUS: EAGLE'S NEST INTEGRITY. OPERATIONS: SECURE RADIO
FREQUENCY ONLY.

HIGH ALERT IN CROWD SITUATIONS: MUST KEEP HANDS OF CIVILIANS
OUTSIDE ARM'S LENGTH OF EAGLE'S NEST AT ALL TIMES. IN THE EVENT
OF BREACH OR NEAR BREACH INVOLVING CITIZEN REACHING IN THE
DIRECTION OF EAGLE'S NEST PRIOR TO ARRANGED SCREENING AND/OR
REHEARSAL OF "PULL GAG," USE OF DEADLY FORCE AUTHORIZED.

NO FURTHER INFORMATION.

Washington Post, October 12, 2018

President Trump chastises a student while speaking to a group of first graders at Phoebe Hearst Elementary School in Washington.

First-graders maul heckler during Trump visit

BY ANTON WALDVOGEL

WASHINGTON—A visit to a local elementary school turned violent Thursday when a group a first graders attacked fellow student Carlson Nunemacher, who interrupted the president's reading of "The Day The Crayons Quit."

The boy suffered minor bruises and scratches, and was rushed to the school nurse's office shortly after the incident.

Some observers expressed concern that President Trump seemed to encourage the crowd of children to be rough with Nunemacher, 6.

Planned as a cordial visit with children to provide a photo-op for the president, the event turned to chaos when Nunemacher interrupted Trump's ad-libbed comments, which he made frequently while reading the book. Nunemacher yelled out, "Those aren't the words, you dummy."

The other children immediately rose to the president's defense, shouting over the boy with chants of "USA, USA, USA!" drowning him out and compelling the president to pause.

Some children shoved the boy. The president, while not acting to control the situation, quietly motioned to his Secret Service detail to escort the child out of the room.

As the Secret Service worked their way through the group of children, President Trump appeared annoyed at being made to wait while agents dealt with the disturbance.

"Get rid of him!" the president suddenly yelled. "Get him the hell out."

This sudden comment stoked the children further, as cheers rose above the jeers and boos, and some children even struck the boy.

"But don't hurt him," The president added quietly as other children continued to cheer, yell, hit the boy, and tear at his clothes.

The children applauded wildly when the boy was removed from the classroom crying.

President Trump continued, "I feel a lot of love in this room. There's something special going on here. The silent majority is not silent anymore."

According to the teacher, Beverly Parker, Trump had set the stage for the aggressive behavior by "whipping the children into a frenzy," prior to the incident.

"He paused a lot while he read and would go off about how everybody should get dessert instead of vegetables at every meal, and stay up all night. The children loved it. They were cheering. He had them eating out of his hand," Parker said.

The president also talked about the teacher during his reading, saying, "Your teacher is not a leader, is she? She's made stupid decisions. And that's why your class doesn't have fun anymore. You have homework and tests. We don't like those, do we?"

The president went on to question the need for teachers, asking the students if they thought all the teachers should be banned from the school, calling them "despicable."

"But I promise I wouldn't kill them. I hate them. I think some of them—many of them—are terrible people—but I would never kill a teacher. That would be wrong."

The president added: "But..." knowingly pausing as if considering the prospect.

"That's when it really got scary," according to Alison Dumound, a teacher's aide assigned to the class. "He was tapping into a very dark place in these children, and they smelled blood in the water."

Trump did not comment on the disturbance, only to indicate that he thought the visit was "very nice."

Students expressed overall approval of the president's visit.

"He says the things we're thinking but we know better not to say, and I really liked that," said student Caroline Thede, 7.

MAKING AMERICA FIT AGAIN

The President's Council on Fitness will be fortified under Trump to ensure American schoolchildren are more physically fit than foreign children. New fitness guidelines based on Donald Trump's own exercise regimen will encourage youths to become almost as fit as the healthiest president to ever hold the office.

FACE CRUNCHES
Contract facial muscles around the eyes and mouth into a stern grimace.

ACCUSATION THROW
Hurl blame with force.

50-FLOOR DASH
Take elevator to the 50th floor as quickly as possible. (Holding the door for others comes out of your time.)

FLEXIBILITY
Become as rigid and inflexible as possible, showing no weak pliability.

ENDURANCE
Remain in the presence of inferior individuals for an extended period. Monitor heart rate.

TRUMP'S HEALTH STATS
Height: 5'10" (6'2" on best hair days)
Weight: Fantastic
Blood: Red (100% American)
Liver: Non-lilied
Cholesterol: Medium rare
Vision: Sees through bullshit
Hearing: Heard what you said about him
Cognition and Logic Skills: Pancakes
Skin: Dry-cleaned twice a week
Money Flaps: 2.5", 3.5" when aroused
Chronic Ailment(s): Billionaire's elbow

Top Trump Tweets

If no one presses the red button, how do we know if it works?

• • •

Trump Creates Presidential Anti-Defamation League

By PATRICK JOHANSON

WASHINGTON — In a signing statement Friday, President Trump created the Presidential Anti-Defamation League as part of the broader Presidential Fairness and Protection Act. Mr. Trump's statement decried the mistreatment of President-Americans and vowed the new agency would "make the forces of hate and injustice accountable."

"Discriminatory slurs like 'President Chump' and 'Insulter in Chief' are directed toward only those who happen to be president," Mr. Trump said in the statement. "Such attacks are a shameful relic of our bigoted past."

The league will work to protect those of presidential origin by establishing stiffer punishments, including prison time, for overtly presidentist remarks that unfairly target anyone in the U.S.-executive-office-holding minority.

The Rev. Garland Hall, a presidential rights attorney, worked with Mr. Trump on the creation of the new rights organization. Said Mr. Hall, "For too long this office has been victimized by the hate and injustice of presidentaphobes. We will overcome."

Last week, Mr. Trump urged Congress to send him a presidential hate-crimes bill to expand protections for people of presidential origin against bias from the media and protesters.

Continued on Page A10

NATHANIEL MORRIS/THE NEW YORK TIMES

The president in the Oval Office with presidential civil rights leaders in January.

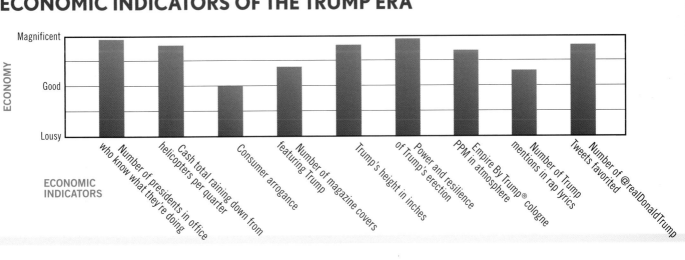

ECONOMIC INDICATORS OF THE TRUMP ERA

ECONOMY — Magnificent / Good / Lousy

ECONOMIC INDICATORS:
- Number of presidents in office who know what they're doing
- Cash total raining down from helicopters per quarter
- Consumer arrogance
- Number of magazine covers featuring Trump
- Trump's height in inches
- Power and resilience of Trump's erection
- PPM in atmosphere
- Empire By Trump® cologne
- Number of Trump mentions in rap lyrics
- Number of @realDonaldTrump Tweets favorited

TRUMP'S CHARIOT: A PRESIDENTIAL RIDE

The presidential motorcade of recent years is only distinguishable from a funeral procession by the color of the flags on the vehicles. If you thought that as the leader of the free world, President Trump would sit in the back seat of a plain black Town Car, think again! President Trump travels in extreme comfort, security, and glory at the helm of his spectacular presidential chariot.

FEATURES

1. Sweet-ass rims
2. Decorative skulls of enemies
3. Cowcatcher attachment for sweeping Popemobiles aside
4. "My other car is a yacht" bumper sticker
5. Sometimes has bulletproof shield, sometimes doesn't, to stay unpredictable
6. Top-notch heating and cooling system that proves global warming is a hoax
7. Headrest contains special seat belt for Trump hair
8. Plenty of room for beauty contestants
9. Self-driving computer system pre-programmed to run over journalists
10. "Hail To The Chief" car horn
11. Ejector seat for undesirable passengers
12. Razor-sharp dollar-sign-shaped hub blades to shred wheels of other chariots
13. Exhaust scented to smell like Success By Trump® cologne
14. Cell charger for uninterrupted tweeting
15. Never-be-captured self-detonation button
16. Mad Max–style punk-band stage
17. Muslim-seeking missile launcher
18. Top speed of 9 billion mph
19. Fireworks launcher
20. Microphones to record any great ideas President Trump has while driving through crowds of poor people
21. Golden-spear ejector
22. Mounted gold piano for Tony Bennett
23. GoPro-sponsored cameras that stream 360° view of Trump in the chariot to worldwide audience

24. NASA space-booster attachments for quick escapes
25. Several big, red buttons
26. Protective coating that keeps out other people's ideas and feelings
27. Magma-proof undercarriage
28. Trailed by film-quality light setup to give Trump a heavenly glow

The Trump Chariot will be burned along with the president in the event of his death, so that he may ride it into the afterlife.

A Look At Every President In American History And Why Trump Trumps Them All

Although singular in the scope and dimension of his reign, President Trump will remain a leader firmly situated within the context of a long line of historic commanders in chief. Having thoroughly skimmed the primary achievements of our nation's past presidents, Trump has found ways to improve upon them all and, in so doing, finally fulfill the promise of their failed legacies.

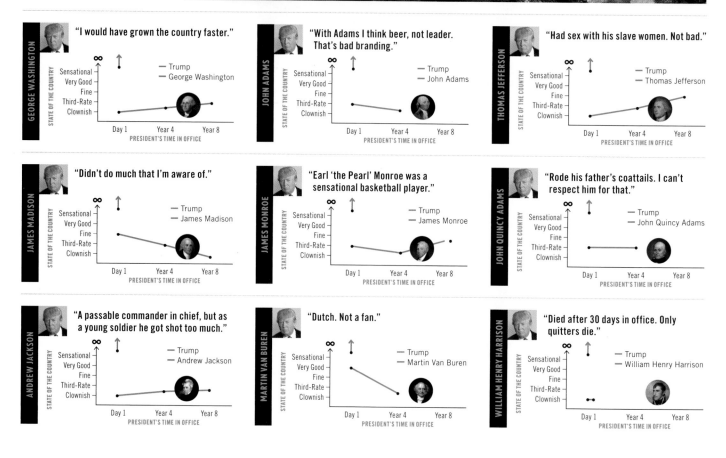

GEORGE WASHINGTON — "I would have grown the country faster."
STATE OF THE COUNTRY: Sensational, Very Good, Fine, Third-Rate, Clownish
— Trump
— George Washington
Day 1, Year 4, Year 8
PRESIDENT'S TIME IN OFFICE

JOHN ADAMS — "With Adams I think beer, not leader. That's bad branding."
STATE OF THE COUNTRY: Sensational, Very Good, Fine, Third-Rate, Clownish
— Trump
— John Adams
Day 1, Year 4, Year 8
PRESIDENT'S TIME IN OFFICE

THOMAS JEFFERSON — "Had sex with his slave women. Not bad."
STATE OF THE COUNTRY: Sensational, Very Good, Fine, Third-Rate, Clownish
— Trump
— Thomas Jefferson
Day 1, Year 4, Year 8
PRESIDENT'S TIME IN OFFICE

JAMES MADISON — "Didn't do much that I'm aware of."
STATE OF THE COUNTRY: Sensational, Very Good, Fine, Third-Rate, Clownish
— Trump
— James Madison
Day 1, Year 4, Year 8
PRESIDENT'S TIME IN OFFICE

JAMES MONROE — "Earl 'the Pearl' Monroe was a sensational basketball player."
STATE OF THE COUNTRY: Sensational, Very Good, Fine, Third-Rate, Clownish
— Trump
— James Monroe
Day 1, Year 4, Year 8
PRESIDENT'S TIME IN OFFICE

JOHN QUINCY ADAMS — "Rode his father's coattails. I can't respect him for that."
STATE OF THE COUNTRY: Sensational, Very Good, Fine, Third-Rate, Clownish
— Trump
— John Quincy Adams
Day 1, Year 4, Year 8
PRESIDENT'S TIME IN OFFICE

ANDREW JACKSON — "A passable commander in chief, but as a young soldier he got shot too much."
STATE OF THE COUNTRY: Sensational, Very Good, Fine, Third-Rate, Clownish
— Trump
— Andrew Jackson
Day 1, Year 4, Year 8
PRESIDENT'S TIME IN OFFICE

MARTIN VAN BUREN — "Dutch. Not a fan."
STATE OF THE COUNTRY: Sensational, Very Good, Fine, Third-Rate, Clownish
— Trump
— Martin Van Buren
Day 1, Year 4, Year 8
PRESIDENT'S TIME IN OFFICE

WILLIAM HENRY HARRISON — "Died after 30 days in office. Only quitters die."
STATE OF THE COUNTRY: Sensational, Very Good, Fine, Third-Rate, Clownish
— Trump
— William Henry Harrison
Day 1, Year 4, Year 8
PRESIDENT'S TIME IN OFFICE

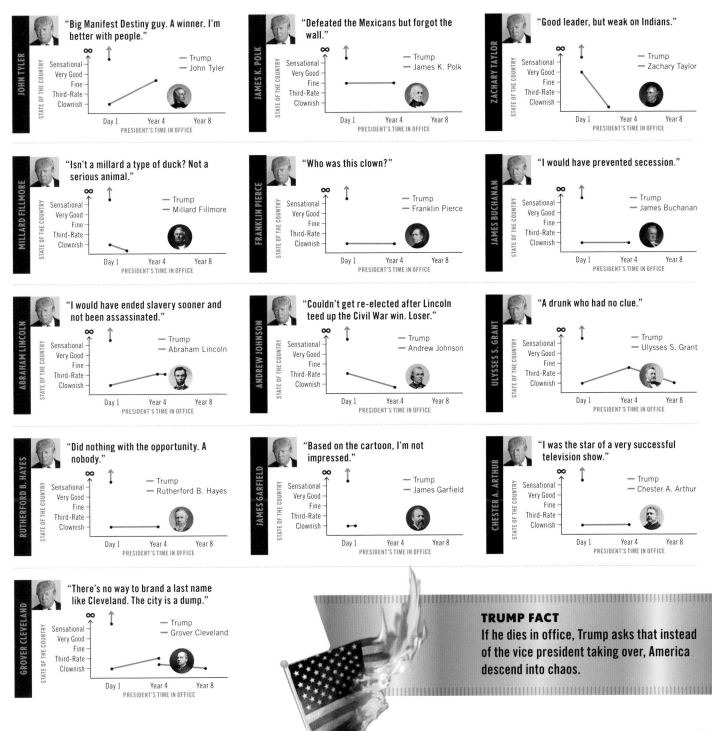

JOHN TYLER — "Big Manifest Destiny guy. A winner. I'm better with people."

JAMES K. POLK — "Defeated the Mexicans but forgot the wall."

ZACHARY TAYLOR — "Good leader, but weak on Indians."

MILLARD FILLMORE — "Isn't a millard a type of duck? Not a serious animal."

FRANKLIN PIERCE — "Who was this clown?"

JAMES BUCHANAN — "I would have prevented secession."

ABRAHAM LINCOLN — "I would have ended slavery sooner and not been assassinated."

ANDREW JOHNSON — "Couldn't get re-elected after Lincoln teed up the Civil War win. Loser."

ULYSSES S. GRANT — "A drunk who had no clue."

RUTHERFORD B. HAYES — "Did nothing with the opportunity. A nobody."

JAMES GARFIELD — "Based on the cartoon, I'm not impressed."

CHESTER A. ARTHUR — "I was the star of a very successful television show."

GROVER CLEVELAND — "There's no way to brand a last name like Cleveland. The city is a dump."

Each chart: STATE OF THE COUNTRY (Sensational, Very Good, Fine, Third-Rate, Clownish) vs PRESIDENT'S TIME IN OFFICE (Day 1, Year 4, Year 8), with legend lines for Trump and the respective president.

TRUMP FACT
If he dies in office, Trump asks that instead of the vice president taking over, America descend into chaos.

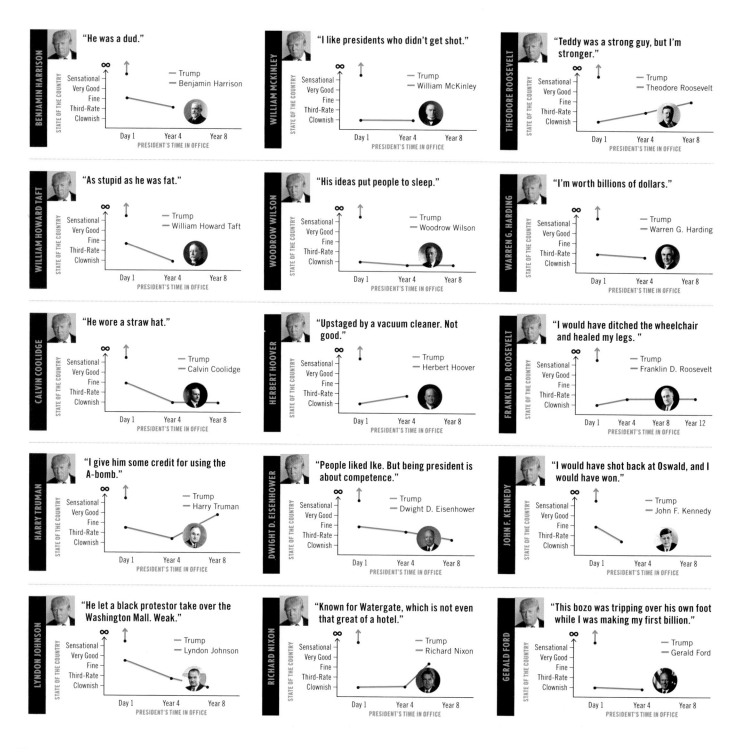

BENJAMIN HARRISON

"He was a dud."

STATE OF THE COUNTRY
Sensational / Very Good / Fine / Third-Rate / Clownish

— Trump
— Benjamin Harrison

Day 1 — Year 4 — Year 8
PRESIDENT'S TIME IN OFFICE

WILLIAM McKINLEY

"I like presidents who didn't get shot."

STATE OF THE COUNTRY
Sensational / Very Good / Fine / Third-Rate / Clownish

— Trump
— William McKinley

Day 1 — Year 4 — Year 8
PRESIDENT'S TIME IN OFFICE

THEODORE ROOSEVELT

"Teddy was a strong guy, but I'm stronger."

STATE OF THE COUNTRY
Sensational / Very Good / Fine / Third-Rate / Clownish

— Trump
— Theodore Roosevelt

Day 1 — Year 4 — Year 8
PRESIDENT'S TIME IN OFFICE

WILLIAM HOWARD TAFT

"As stupid as he was fat."

STATE OF THE COUNTRY
Sensational / Very Good / Fine / Third-Rate / Clownish

— Trump
— William Howard Taft

Day 1 — Year 4 — Year 8
PRESIDENT'S TIME IN OFFICE

WOODROW WILSON

"His ideas put people to sleep."

STATE OF THE COUNTRY
Sensational / Very Good / Fine / Third-Rate / Clownish

— Trump
— Woodrow Wilson

Day 1 — Year 4 — Year 8
PRESIDENT'S TIME IN OFFICE

WARREN G. HARDING

"I'm worth billions of dollars."

STATE OF THE COUNTRY
Sensational / Very Good / Fine / Third-Rate / Clownish

— Trump
— Warren G. Harding

Day 1 — Year 4 — Year 8
PRESIDENT'S TIME IN OFFICE

CALVIN COOLIDGE

"He wore a straw hat."

STATE OF THE COUNTRY
Sensational / Very Good / Fine / Third-Rate / Clownish

— Trump
— Calvin Coolidge

Day 1 — Year 4 — Year 8
PRESIDENT'S TIME IN OFFICE

HERBERT HOOVER

"Upstaged by a vacuum cleaner. Not good."

STATE OF THE COUNTRY
Sensational / Very Good / Fine / Third-Rate / Clownish

— Trump
— Herbert Hoover

Day 1 — Year 4 — Year 8
PRESIDENT'S TIME IN OFFICE

FRANKLIN D. ROOSEVELT

"I would have ditched the wheelchair and healed my legs. "

STATE OF THE COUNTRY
Sensational / Very Good / Fine / Third-Rate / Clownish

— Trump
— Franklin D. Roosevelt

Day 1 — Year 4 — Year 8 — Year 12
PRESIDENT'S TIME IN OFFICE

HARRY TRUMAN

"I give him some credit for using the A-bomb."

STATE OF THE COUNTRY
Sensational / Very Good / Fine / Third-Rate / Clownish

— Trump
— Harry Truman

Day 1 — Year 4 — Year 8
PRESIDENT'S TIME IN OFFICE

DWIGHT D. EISENHOWER

"People liked Ike. But being president is about competence."

STATE OF THE COUNTRY
Sensational / Very Good / Fine / Third-Rate / Clownish

— Trump
— Dwight D. Eisenhower

Day 1 — Year 4 — Year 8
PRESIDENT'S TIME IN OFFICE

JOHN F. KENNEDY

"I would have shot back at Oswald, and I would have won."

STATE OF THE COUNTRY
Sensational / Very Good / Fine / Third-Rate / Clownish

— Trump
— John F. Kennedy

Day 1 — Year 4 — Year 8
PRESIDENT'S TIME IN OFFICE

LYNDON JOHNSON

"He let a black protestor take over the Washington Mall. Weak."

STATE OF THE COUNTRY
Sensational / Very Good / Fine / Third-Rate / Clownish

— Trump
— Lyndon Johnson

Day 1 — Year 4 — Year 8
PRESIDENT'S TIME IN OFFICE

RICHARD NIXON

"Known for Watergate, which is not even that great of a hotel."

STATE OF THE COUNTRY
Sensational / Very Good / Fine / Third-Rate / Clownish

— Trump
— Richard Nixon

Day 1 — Year 4 — Year 8
PRESIDENT'S TIME IN OFFICE

GERALD FORD

"This bozo was tripping over his own foot while I was making my first billion."

STATE OF THE COUNTRY
Sensational / Very Good / Fine / Third-Rate / Clownish

— Trump
— Gerald Ford

Day 1 — Year 4 — Year 8
PRESIDENT'S TIME IN OFFICE

PRESIDENT TRUMP: AMERICA'S NEW BOSS

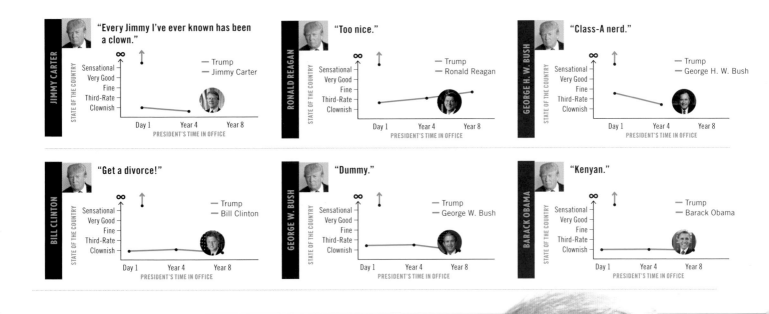

JIMMY CARTER — "Every Jimmy I've ever known has been a clown."

STATE OF THE COUNTRY: Sensational / Very Good / Fine / Third-Rate / Clownish
— Trump
— Jimmy Carter
PRESIDENT'S TIME IN OFFICE: Day 1 / Year 4 / Year 8

RONALD REAGAN — "Too nice."

STATE OF THE COUNTRY: Sensational / Very Good / Fine / Third-Rate / Clownish
— Trump
— Ronald Reagan
PRESIDENT'S TIME IN OFFICE: Day 1 / Year 4 / Year 8

GEORGE H. W. BUSH — "Class-A nerd."

STATE OF THE COUNTRY: Sensational / Very Good / Fine / Third-Rate / Clownish
— Trump
— George H. W. Bush
PRESIDENT'S TIME IN OFFICE: Day 1 / Year 4 / Year 8

BILL CLINTON — "Get a divorce!"

STATE OF THE COUNTRY: Sensational / Very Good / Fine / Third-Rate / Clownish
— Trump
— Bill Clinton
PRESIDENT'S TIME IN OFFICE: Day 1 / Year 4 / Year 8

GEORGE W. BUSH — "Dummy."

STATE OF THE COUNTRY: Sensational / Very Good / Fine / Third-Rate / Clownish
— Trump
— George W. Bush
PRESIDENT'S TIME IN OFFICE: Day 1 / Year 4 / Year 8

BARACK OBAMA — "Kenyan."

STATE OF THE COUNTRY: Sensational / Very Good / Fine / Third-Rate / Clownish
— Trump
— Barack Obama
PRESIDENT'S TIME IN OFFICE: Day 1 / Year 4 / Year 8

WHITE HOUSE STAFFERS WHO TOTALLY WON'T BE COERCED INTO SAYING TRUMP IS A NICE GUY

👍 President Trump's robot butler

👍 The White House Yes Man

👍 Bernard, the Senior Science Advisor who just needs to fly under the radar until retirement

👍 Senior Advisor whose date-rape charge is about to go away

👍 Visiting Estonian dignitary who looks an awful lot like Melania in drag

👍 Akmed Rahmed, Head of Muslim Relations/Staff Prisoner

👍 Bust of Abraham Lincoln

👍 Danish White House tourist phonetically reading "Trump is a nice guy" from a cue card

DATE: February 16, 2017
FROM: President Donald Trump <DTRUMP@WHITEHOUSE.GOV>
TO: Major General George J. Franz III <GJFRANZ@USARMY.GOV>
SUBJECT: CONTENTS OF CRATE #9906755

Major General Franz,

As the newly elected president it's my duty to protect the people. We have a lot of enemies out there who are laughing at us and want to destroy us. The Chinese, ISIS, the Russians, and the illegal immigrants, just to name a few.

For this reason, I'm ordering the Intelligence Branch of the United States Army to retrieve Crate #9906755 from its top-secret location. I've known about the existence of this crate for a long time. We've kept it hidden, and for what? Now is the time to reveal this fabulous weapon to our enemies.

It's time to release the ARK OF THE COVENANT

I realize it's a dangerous artifact, and in the wrong hands, it could do irreparable damage, yadda yadda yadda. But with these big threats we're facing and all of these people waiting to take a shot at us, we have no choice.

I've spoken to the top men — really, the very best guys — and they tell me that if we open the Ark now, our army will be invincible — so strong that no one will mess with us.

Deliver the crate to the White House this afternoon, and provide me with the proper rabbinic robes and headdress for the opening ritual.

Some have said that there may be a risk to me in opening the Ark and looking inside. I don't think so. I rebuilt Atlantic City. I can handle opening a box.

Sincerely,

President Trump

TRUMP FACT
President Trump demands all White House tourists be provided with guns for added security.

Trump to serve as grand marshal for every U.S. parade

President will take over candy throwing

Everett Dietz
USA TODAY

WASHINGTON In a new initiative designed to improve what he calls the "sad and very poor" quality of parades nationwide, President Trump signed an executive order Monday stipulating that all parades will feature Trump as grand marshal. His duties will include kicking off parades, throwing candy from leading floats, and ensuring that the parade presents a "fun and dazzling spectacle worthy of an American parade."

According to the executive order, the effort will give parades the credibility and competence they could not otherwise achieve under their current leadership, which Trump called "a hodgepodge of unreliable or drunken clowns."

Parades covered under the new order include only those celebrating American holidays, patriotism, American business, American products, approved cultures, American intervention in foreign wars, and President Trump himself. All parades are to take place within the city where President

CLAY SEYMOUR, GETTY IMAGES

President Trump presiding over the Radish Days Parade in McKlusky, ND. Similar parades across the country are now mandated to be led by Trump.

> ## "A truly great country needs truly great parades."
>
> President **Donald Trump**

Trump happens to be at any given time and are subject to being relocated and rescheduled for the president's convenience. All residents of towns in which parades are scheduled will be required to attend.

Several regiments of U.S. soldiers as well as local National Guardsmen are to be provided to each parade to march in formation. Armed nuclear missiles, if located in silos within 100 miles from the parade route, are required to be removed and transported by the morning of the parade and displayed on large flatbed trucks as part of the procession.

The White House Domestic Policy Council estimates the president will spend roughly 135 days every year fulfilling his new grand-marshal duties.

Top Trump Tweets

.@andybass822
Your tweet attacking me made no sense. You have 14 followers so nobody cares. You're trash.

IN THIS TEMPLE
AS IN THE HEARTS OF THE PEOPLE
FOR WHOM HE SAVED THE UNION
THE MEMORY OF DONALD TRUMP
IS ENSHRINED FOREVER

GOVERNMENT

OF THE GOOD PEOPLE, BY THE GOOD PEOPLE, AND FOR THE GOOD PEOPLE

PRESIDENT TRUMP'S CABINET
The Second-Smartest People In The Room

Every great leader needs great people around him. No one knows this better than Donald Trump, who is close friends with some of the greatest people in business, law, reality TV, and hair care. That's why as president, he has filled his cabinet with only the smartest, most successful—and great—people.

Vice President
Chewbacca

Secretary of State
Member of Kiss (any)

Defense Secretary
Clubber Lang

Secretary of Wrestling
Vince McMahon

Attorney General
Rihanna

Secretary of Interior Design
Martha Stewart

Secretary of Pizza
Papa John

Chief of Staff
The ShamWow Guy

Chief of Carl Icahn
Carl Icahn

SUPREME COURT NOMINEES
Justices Who Aren't Dummies

President Trump will nominate only the most qualified and least stupid jurists to the nation's highest court.

Judge Dredd

The Resuscitated Corpse of Evel Knievel

A beautiful woman

Tai Lopez

The Trump Organization, Inc.

NEW GOVERNMENT AGENCIES

Trump has promised to shrink the overall size of government, slashing budgets and eliminating useless bureaucracies like, for example, the Department of Justice. But some new departments need to be created to truly make America great again.

Department of Housing and Luxury Development

Department of Helicopter Valets

The Environmental Baloney Agency

Department of Getting All The Oil

Department of Many Smart People

Department of Great Deals

Bureau of Trump Grandkids' Hot Babysitters

The Office of Civil Rights and How to Stop Whining About Them

Department of Wall

Army Corps of Less Nerdy Engineers

National Registry of Historic Trump Towers

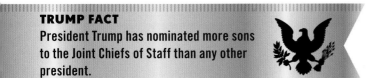

TRUMP FACT
President Trump has nominated more sons to the Joint Chiefs of Staff than any other president.

WOMEN'S HEALTH MENSTRUATION AND WEIGHT COUNCIL

Women 18–35 are required to appear before President Trump and his appointed judges to undergo a series of tests to determine where they need improvement. (Women over 35 are exempt from the procedure.)

An Agency of the U.S. Department of Women's Physical and Mental Fitness

Mission: To make America's women beautiful again.

Physical Fitness Exam: Measurements followed by constructive-criticism sessions and jiggle test.

Mandatory Meal Plans: Customized to suit body problem areas, predominantly diet-pill based.

Personality/IQ Test: To determine which lady-jobs are most suitable.

Psychological Assessment: Crying rooms, tissues, Midol, and birth-control pills will be provided to reduce mood swings/abdominal swelling. Women will state their feelings, receive President Trump's solution, and move on.

Noncompliance with council recommendations will result in a fine of $100,000 and five years in federal prison.

Meet the Administrator
Donald Trump, Administrator
The leading authority on feminine physical and mental health, committed to ensuring that America's female population takes advantage of his expertise.

A BETTER, SMARTER IRS

Get ready for some big changes when it comes to taxes. We'll have new tax brackets, for starters. And whether you're in the Loser tax bracket or the Total Loser tax bracket, you'll benefit from Trump's tax plan for America. You'll especially benefit if you're in the Rich, Super Rich, Billionaire, Super-Billionaire, or Trump tax bracket. (You are not in the Trump bracket.) Here are just a few of the other new tax laws you can look forward to:

★ Taxes will be paid by mailing gold bricks directly to the IRS. If you have run out of gold bricks, payment is also accepted in Rolls-Royces, hotels, or eastern-European models.

★ You may claim up to three golf courses as dependents.

★ Check box 110-a if you would like your tax refund to be reinvested into the Trump real-estate portfolio. (Checking box 110-a is mandatory.)

★ If you earned any income in Mexico during the current fiscal year, a representative from the Deportation Force will be in touch with you shortly.

★ If you earned any income in China during the current fiscal year, check box 13-b, which states, "I wish to donate my entire adjusted gross income to the U.S. Treasury."

★ Income from writing a best-selling business book qualifies for a deduction, pending President Trump's review.

★ If you have been sued by the president this year, be sure to mark that in box 48-f.

★ If you are a woman between the ages of 16 and 21, please remember to attach an 8"x10" glossy headshot with your tax return.

★ Haircuts may be counted as a business expense. Looking good is half of making the deal.

★ If you find yourself being audited, don't panic. Simply remember that whatever happens to you, President Trump will be just fine.

Where Your Tax Dollars Go In A Trump Administration

- **$.8 billion**: Sewn together to make presidential hammock
- **$16 billion**: Casinos in every state-capitol building
- **$3.7 billion**: White House fallout shelter/casino
- **$8 billion**: Sent into outer space after being signed by Trump
- **$5 billion**: Ivanka's anti-aging serum
- **$14.1 billion**: Building a second White House made of money
- **$2.2 billion**: President Trump's escape pod

Bureau of Labor Statistics Report: 'Trump Keeps Knocking Reports Out of Our Hands'

By BRADLEY SCHROEDER

WASHINGTON — The Bureau of Labor Statistics reported today that President Trump repeatedly knocks reports out of their hands. The report showed the frequency of incursions was consistent, regardless of the nature of the report or the time of day it's carried by agency personnel through hallways of government buildings.

"President Trump always seems to find us whenever we've released a new report," said Albert Haberstroh, the department's secretary who coauthored the report.

From a department-wide study citing reported instances of incursions by Mr. Trump, the emerging pattern, according to department analysts, consists of Mr. Trump advancing "seeming-

ly from nowhere" to quickly slap the report to the ground, causing papers to fly about and scatter. The report adds, "The president typically laughs hardily after each occurrence." Additional incidents have involved the president pointing at something in the distance, saying, "What's that?" then grabbing the report and running away.

The agency found a slightly higher probability the president would knock a report out of their hands if it was contained in a folder, unbound. "We believe this provided the president with more papers to be strewn across the floor," Haberstroh said.

According to the report, 65 percent of instances involving loose paper resulted in the president ordering the department official to pick up all the papers. Said the secretary: "Very often he has admonished us for being 'clumsy,' or

JULIA YU FOR THE NEW YORK TIMES

Bureau of Labor Statistics Secretary Albert Haberstroh addresses senior staff today to discuss strategies for evading Trump.

'messing up his hallway' despite the fact that we were not at fault." The report noted Mr. Trump's key advisors or cabinet members frequently snicker alongside him during the encounters.

Based on key findings, the study projects a statistical trend in the next fiscal year in which upcoming reports on wage changes and new unemployment figures

will result in more incursions, including Mr. Trump writing "kick me" on a piece of paper and taping it to the bureau undersecretary's back.

On Tuesday, Secretary Haberstroh presented the report to Mr. Trump and he slapped it to the floor.

The As

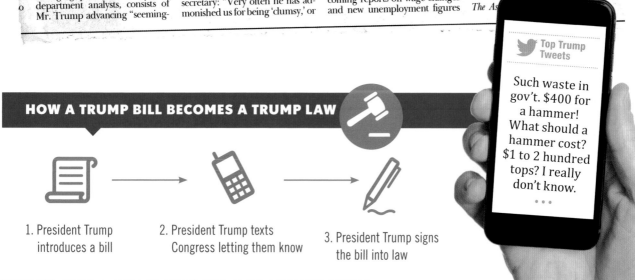

HOW A TRUMP BILL BECOMES A TRUMP LAW

1. President Trump introduces a bill

2. President Trump texts Congress letting them know

3. President Trump signs the bill into law

Top Trump Tweets

Such waste in gov't. $400 for a hammer! What should a hammer cost? $1 to 2 hundred tops? I really don't know.

• • •

Introducing The Trumptitution

Trump's Edits To The "Overrated" U.S. Constitution

While a great and noble document, the U.S. Constitution has its share of flaws. It was written by men who neither graduated from the Wharton School of Business nor read *Crippled America*. An expert at fixing bad contracts, President Trump will pen some necessary edits to America's founding document.

TRUMP FACT
The Bill of Rights is an important list of our Founding Fathers' suggestions.

We the People

PREAMBLES ARE FOR PEOPLE WHO GET PAID BY THE WORD. CUT.

AMERICA IS GETTING LAUGHED AT AND PUSHED AROUND. WHERE IS THE COMMON DEFENSE FOR THAT?

A LAWYER NEEDS TO LOOK AT THIS. I'VE GOT THE BEST LEGAL PEOPLE IN THE WORLD WORKING FOR ME.

ENGLISH PLEASE.

SO MUCH OF THIS IS OUTDATED AND HOKEY!

WORDY!

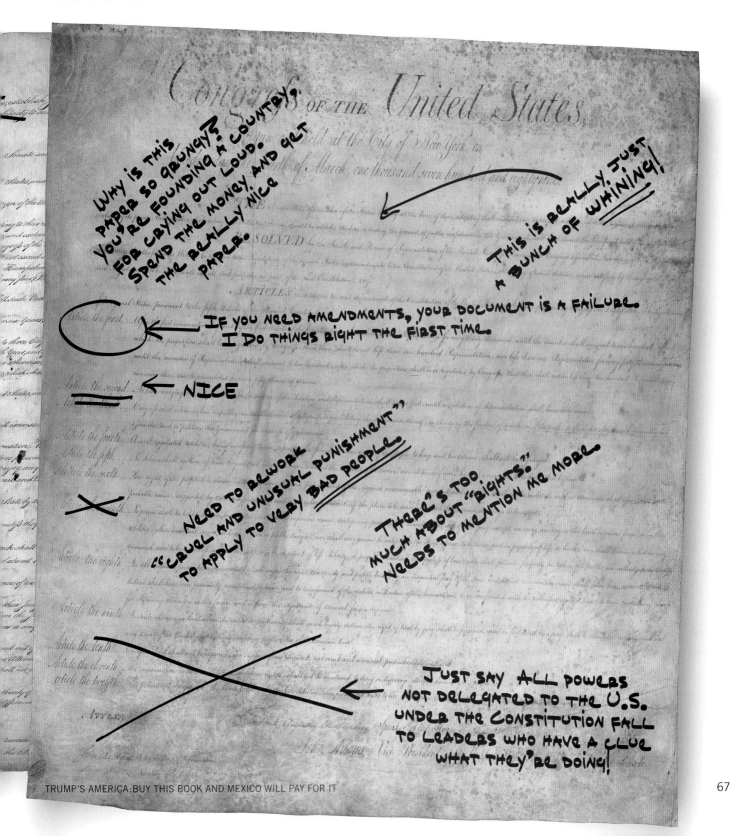

WHAT'S WITH ALL THE SECTIONS AND ARTICLES? WE GET IT! THE STATES ANSWER TO THE PRESIDENT, AND THE CONGRESS AND JUDICIARY ARE USELESS.

ONLY NERDS ARE READING.

THIS PART IS GOOD, WHERE IT SAYS I'M IN CHARGE OF ARMY AND NAVY. MOVE THAT UP HIGHER. (+ UPDATE WITH AIR FORCE, SPACE FORCE, ROBOT FORCE...)

NEED TO INSERT ARTICLE: "THE RIGHT TO KEEP AND OWN GOLF COURSES IN TIMES OF PEACE AND WAR, NO MATTER HOW STRATEGIC THE LOCATION."

Article III.

"I, THE LEADER OF THE UNITED STATES OF AMERICA, IN ORDER TO MAKE AMERICA GREAT AGAIN, DO SOLEMNLY SIGN THIS DEAL TO BRING SWIFT JUSTICE TO ISIS, SEND HOME ALL THE BAD PEOPLE, BUILD A WALL, AND GIVE EVERY AMERICAN A GUN, GOD BLESS THE NEW AND IMPROVED UNITED STATES OF TRUMP'S AMERICA..." THAT'S ALL YOU NEED HERE.

Article IV.

Top Trump Tweets

There are 435 legislators in the House of Reps. By my count only 3 even remotely bangable. Sad!

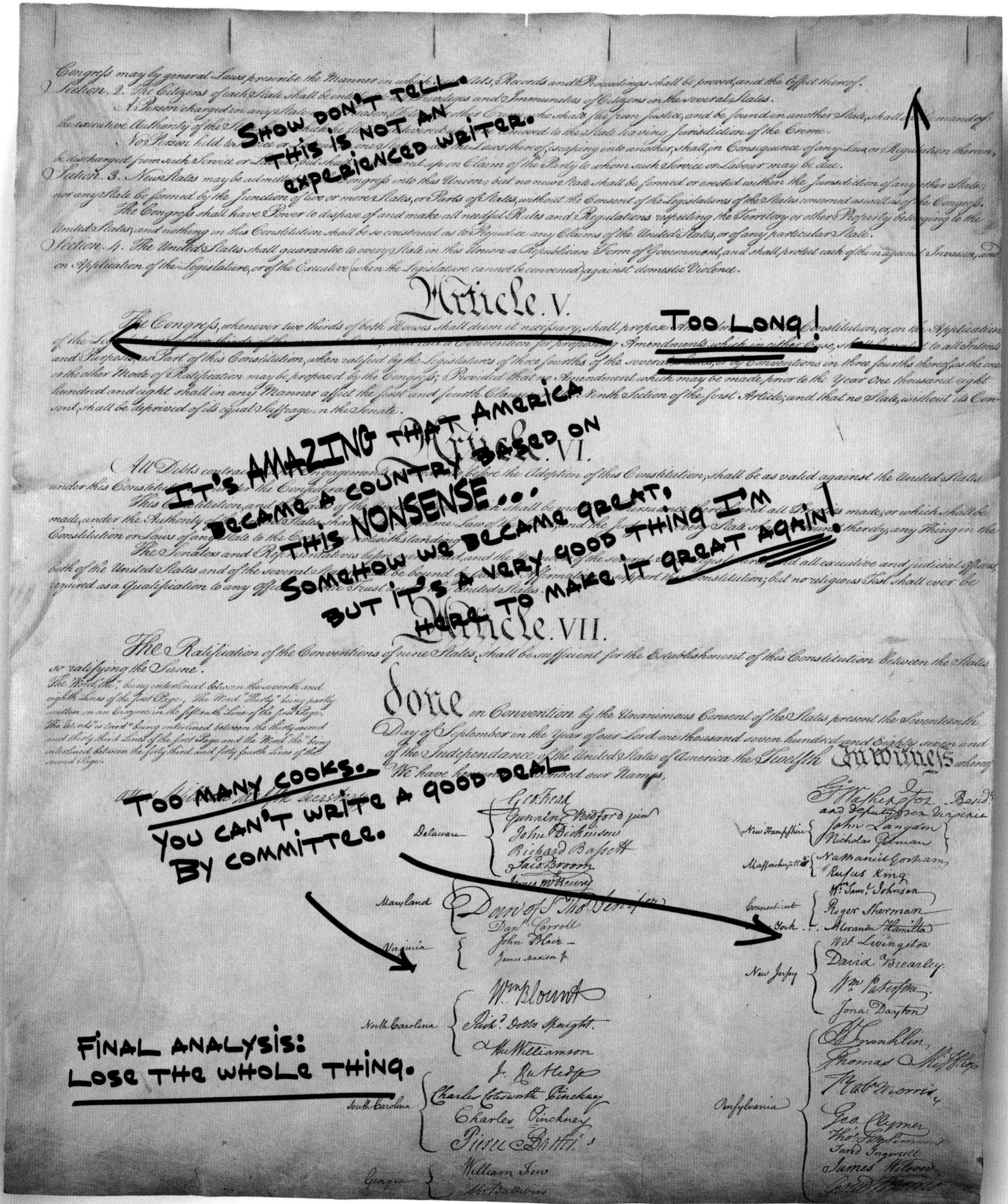
SHOW DON'T TELL.
THIS IS NOT AN EXPERIENCED WRITER.
TOO LONG!
IT'S AMAZING THAT AMERICA BECAME A COUNTRY BASED ON THIS NONSENSE...
SOMEHOW WE BECAME GREAT, BUT IT'S A VERY GOOD THING I'M HERE TO MAKE IT GREAT AGAIN!
TOO MANY COOKS.
YOU CAN'T WRITE A GOOD DEAL BY COMMITTEE.
FINAL ANALYSIS:
LOSE THE WHOLE THING.

The Wall Street Journal, February 22, 2019

Agriculture Secretary Rebuked for Not Giving Food-Safety Briefing 'Any God-Damned Showmanship'

BY ELIZABETH KOZDIAK AND PETER E. HINES

WASHINGTON–Agriculture Secretary Ronald Schwartzman was taken to task by President Trump Wednesday

Ronald Schwartzman

after a "zero pizzazz" annual food safety briefing in the Oval Office. Said the president, "I told him, 'All the bananas in America could be poisoned and I would have no idea, be-

cause you can't seem to keep my attention for more than one second.'"

The agriculture secretary reportedly began the briefing by presenting several facts and statistics, then proceeded to a list of recommendations. "No zing," Mr. Trump said.

Tensions have mounted at the White House in recent weeks, as several cabinet members have failed to spice up key in-person meetings with Mr. Trump. The secretary of education's request for more funding was "out-of-this-world boring," according to White House Press Secretary Bret Michaels, and the attorney general's summary of recent hate crimes was "a snooze-fest."

At a meeting scheduled for tomorrow with FEMA Director Allen Thorsberg to discuss the decimation of Miami from a Category 5 hurricane, the president is expected to look away while doing a hand-job motion.

THE MONEY

TRUMP FACT

Trump's Congress is the only one in U.S. history capable of a four-thirds vote.

LOSER STATES THAT WILL GET NEW NAMES

Many U.S. states are not doing well. As President Trump will demonstrate, this is primarily a problem of branding. Some simple name changes will add some much-needed excitement and class to key loser states.

DONALD TRUMPTANA
Old State Animal: The grizzly bear
New State Animal: Mike Ditka's 1985 Bears
Old State Nickname: The Treasure State
New State Nickname: Trump Gaming Presents: The Treasure State

TRUMPSYLVANIA
Old State Motto: Virtue, Liberty, and Independence
New State Motto: Think Big!
Old State Aircraft: Piper Cub, the plane that looks like a paper airplane
New State Aircraft: The AC-130 Spectre gunship

IVANKOWA
State Rock: Geode
New State Rock: Kid Rock

"Under Ivanka, Ivankowa will become a style leader and business maestro while still being undeniably sexy. If our founding fathers weren't its father, they'd totally date Ivankowa."

DONALWARE
Old State Motto: Liberty and Independence
New Motto: Real estate
Old State Beverage: Milk
New State Beverage: Trump Appletini
Old State Flag: Two bozos between a symbol
New State Flag: The Trump Phoenix

OTHER STATES
Ivanaho
Milaneabama
New Trumpshire
South Donkota
Michigreat

TRUMP'S FAVORITE CAPITAL-PUNISHMENT METHODS

Crushed by Trump's net worth in pennies

Getting "fired" with flamethrower

Lethal Erection

Death by tanning bed

Boiling gold poured into mouth

Sent to Trump's sons' elite private game reserve

Ordered to fight in Trump's Arena

Bludgeoned by *The Art of the Deal*

Torn apart by Trump's rabid Hispanic fan base

Top Trump Tweets

My education platform: Teachers should be 1.) armed with M16s 2.) hot.

• • •

FINALLY, REAL MONEY

Most U.S. currency is too small to be useful, such as the $100 bill. Thankfully, the U.S. Mint under President Trump will introduce the $1 billion note. Finally, America's billionaires can take part in the wonderful American financial system from which they've long been excluded. They can now buy that nuclear submarine, truckload of diamonds, or tropical-island fortress they've always wanted—with the cash in their pocket.

THE NEW TRUMP CITIZENSHIP TEST

Immigration is one of America's greatest security threats. The wall along our Mexican border will be the first line of defense against illegal immigration. The second is the U.S. citizenship test, which asks people to prove they belong where we live.

U.S. Citizenship and Immigration Services

2017 CITIZENSHIP EXAM (revised)

1. In your native un-American country, which income bracket best describes yours?

   (A)   Billionaire
   (B)   Millionaire
   (C)   Huddled masses

2. Are you from Mexico? (Y/N) __. If yes, describe what makes you one of the good ones.

   _____

   _____

3. In a sentence or two, prove that you are not a Muslim.

   _____

   _____

4. Are you from eastern Europe? (Y/N)__. If yes, are you a woman? (Y/N) __. If yes, have you done any modeling? (Y/N) __. If yes, that's very interesting. Would you like to have dinner with the President? (Y/N) __. If yes, I will pick you up at 8.

5. Are you from a country not mentioned previously? (Y/N) __. If yes, why hasn't America heard of it?

   _____

   _____

6. Please list the American jobs you plan to steal:

   _____

   _____

7. Are you Native American? (Y/N) __. If yes, which games least favor the house?

   _____

U.S. Citizenship and Immigration Services

8. Name the three branches of government.

1. _____ 2. _____ 3. _____

9. Name the one that matters.

_____

10. Name the first U.S. president.

_____

11. Name the first U.S. president who matters.

_____

12. Name the top three Trump children.

1. _____ 2. _____ 3. _____

13. How beautiful did you find the wall?

_____

14. In what year did the U.S. officially become so huge and fabulous you've never seen a country like this before and it will make your head spin?

_____

_____

15. Complete the sentence.

   English is my _____ language.

   (A) first
   (B) favorite
   (C) all of the above

16. Did you know President Trump is worth billions? (Y/N) ___.

USA Today, August 24, 2017

...I'm going to do.

Ambassador from Ecuador tipped $2 for 'extra hustle'

Raymond Ellis
USA TODAY

WASHINGTON – In what has become a common practice since Donald Trump took office, the president tipped Ecuadorian Ambassador to the U.S. Guillermo Villagrán two dollars on Thursday, citing his appreciation for Mr. Villagrán's "extra hustle."

"I saw him waiting outside the Oval Office five minutes early and wanted to let him know I appreciated it," President Trump said. "His next cup of coffee is on me."

Mr. Villagrán is the most recent in a series of officials who have become beneficiaries of the president's gratuities. U.K. Prime Minister Theresa May received a five-dollar bill from Mr. Trump after she held the door open for him before at a recent G8 Summit in Brussels.

"These kids are doing a sensational job, they really are," the president said. "If they keep it up, there's more where that came from."

Sources close to the president report that he approves of the recent performance of Pope Francis as well. On the way out of a lengthy private meeting in the Oval Office, Trump is said to have folded an undisclosed amount of cash, slipped it into the Pontiff's hand during a handshake, and told him to "get something nice."

TRUMP'S NEXT GREAT BUSINESS SUCCESS: YOUR HEALTH

Say good riddance to Obamacare and give a warm welcome to TrumpCare®. Making sure the health of every American with the right kind of ethnicity and net worth is taken care of is one of President Trump's top priorities. Look for this TrumpCare brochure in your mailbox soon after his first day in office.

Really Great

TrumpCare® is better than Obamacare, and you'll love it because it's terrific. Designed by Donald Trump himself, TrumpCare® will provide the American people with the health coverage they deserve.

Plan Specifics

✓ It's something wonderful
✓ It's better than Obamacare
✓ So great
✓ Trump knows many doctors—the best in the world—and they all agree that TrumpCare® is incredible
✓ Obamacare bad
✓ Trump!

For-Profit Care

TrumpCare® will not be expensive like Obamacare. In fact, TrumpCare® will actually make a profit.*

*Donald Trump will personally receive a non-negotiable 15% share of all TrumpCare® profits

TrumpCare® comes in three tiers designed to fit your budget, lifestyle, and status.

PlatinumCare®

World-class health care for Americans who make more than $1 billion per year. (Ask your account-ing team if you qualify.)

✓ Gourmet hospital Jello
✓ Top-shelf rubbing alcohol
✓ Emergency-room helicopter rides
✓ Caribbean Burn Unit Cruise
✓ Morphine bar
✓ VIP hospital gowns that close in the back
✓ Gold-lined bed pans
✓ All nurses a Trump-certified 10

"My daughter's emergency-room surgeon was a Muslim. They got rid of him, no questions asked."

CrapCare®

An inexpensive plan for losers.

✓ Group physicals
✓ If you're shot you get to keep the gun
✓ Nurses at least a 4
✓ Complimentary Advil (limit 2)
✓ Private rooms for police interrogation

"When Dad got Alzheimer's, CrapCare® gave me choices, and I chose the Neglect™ option and started living my life again."

"With BasicCare®, I got my parking validated."

BasicCare®

BasicCare® is for those who bring in a low six-figure salary and are fine with that.

✓ Free continental breakfast with cancer diagnosis
✓ Visit from WWE Heavyweight Champion John Cena (subject to substitutions due to wrestling schedule)

TrumpCare®
Health Care That's Great.™

TRUMP FACT
The federal government is the country's biggest employer of morons.

★ ★ ★ TRUMPCARE® QUICK-START GUIDE ★ ★ ★

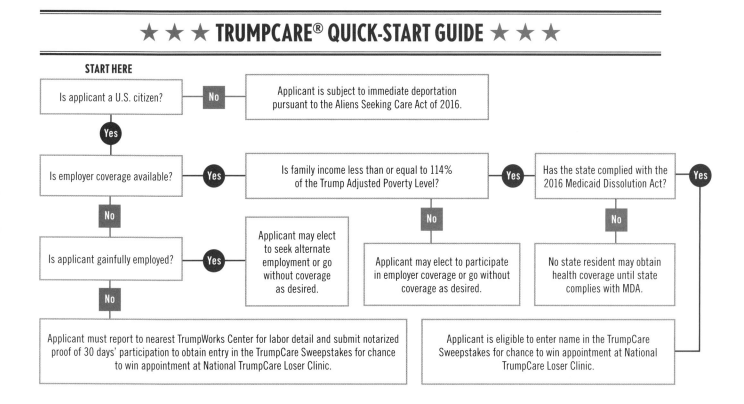

START HERE

Is applicant a U.S. citizen? — **No** → Applicant is subject to immediate deportation pursuant to the Aliens Seeking Care Act of 2016.

Yes ↓

Is employer coverage available? — **Yes** → Is family income less than or equal to 114% of the Trump Adjusted Poverty Level? — **Yes** → Has the state complied with the 2016 Medicaid Dissolution Act? — **Yes**

No ↓

Is applicant gainfully employed? — **Yes** → Applicant may elect to seek alternate employment or go without coverage as desired.

No (income) → Applicant may elect to participate in employer coverage or go without coverage as desired.

No (Medicaid) → No state resident may obtain health coverage until state complies with MDA.

No ↓

Applicant must report to nearest TrumpWorks Center for labor detail and submit notarized proof of 30 days' participation to obtain entry in the TrumpCare Sweepstakes for chance to win appointment at National TrumpCare Loser Clinic.

Applicant is eligible to enter name in the TrumpCare Sweepstakes for chance to win appointment at National TrumpCare Loser Clinic.

TRUMPCARE *For Her*®

Women's health care is so important to Trump, he's created TrumpCare For Her®, a separate brand just for the ladies. TrumpCare For Her not only takes care of women, it cherishes them.

✳ All breast-cancer diagnoses come with a bouquet of flowers
✳ Doctors assure you "my other patients mean nothing to me"
✳ Doctors trained to truly *listen* to your health concerns (but provide the same answers regardless)
✳ Pink needles
✳ Bills printed on perfumed paper with added sheet of invitation tissue

INSIDE YOUR BROCHURE

♥ Understanding your official TrumpCare For Her® Breast Grade

♥ Your "lady parts" checkup schedule

TRUMP: "I don't pretend to know what they do down there at these checkups, but believe me, they're covered big-league."

THE MILITARY

"ARE THESE THE BIGGEST MISSILES WE HAVE?"

INSIDE THE TWITTER WAR ROOM

In 21st century America, the gravest decision a leader makes is whether to declare Twitter war.

Every modern president faces the grim prospect of sending young American characters— sometimes as many as 140—to write on the field of battle, and sometimes make the ultimate sacrifice by being deleted in the line of duty.

In Twitter wartime, we need a commander in chief with the experience and track record to win.

Donald Trump is that president.

To lead tweets in combat, we have in President Trump a seasoned veteran who has served with distinction in multiple Twitter wars, including the Rosie O'Donnell Campaign of 2011, the Battle of Cher's Surgery, and the Second Deadspin War. In conflict after conflict, he has proven himself a masterful literary strategist whose relentless Twitter offensives leave the opposing force broken, silent, and humiliated in the eyes of its followers.

With bravery and resolve, secure in the knowledge the American people will not unfollow him, President Trump considers every option at his disposal, including personal attacks, counter-insults, and even, as a last resort, the F-bomb.

Consider this all-too-real scenario: It is 3 a.m. and the president is awakened by a Twitter alert on his red smartphone. A sitcom writer– producer has gone rogue and is threatening to unleash inflammatory content that will result in serious notifications. The president calls for an immediate Twitter war-room meeting with his top social-media strategists and the Joint Tweets. The experts tell him that, according to the most up-to-date hashtag analyses, an international Twitter incident is imminent. How will President Trump respond? Given the gravity of the situation, we must trust he will tweet decisively, with the safety and Twitter-account security of our nation in his thoughts and tweets.

Inside the Twitter war room, President Trump will never rest. He bears the strong and steady hand of @realDonaldTrump, building a coalition of mentions, favoriting our allies, launching surgical strikes against tyrannical talk-show hosts, and keeping our nation's reserve Twitter warriors in a state of retweet readiness. One thing we can be sure of is that in the annals of Twitter war history, President Donald Trump will proudly stand and answer the call of "What's happening?"

TRUMP'S SECRET PLAN TO DEFEAT ISIS

One day, Donald Trump's covert ISIS strategy will be fully declassified. And that day will come only after the plan's clear and decisive implementation succeeds in exterminating from God's Earth every last tendril of ISIS and all who pay them tribute. Until then, select citizens have access to this redacted copy. As one of those citizens, you must remember the most important weapon in any commander in chief's arsenal is secrecy. So, don't show this to anyone from ISIS!

THE WHITE HOUSE
WASHINGTON

TOP SECRET

FROM THE DESK OF PRESIDENT DONALD J. TRUMP, 45ᵗʰ President, United States of America; Commander-in-Chief, United States Military; Chairman and President, the Trump Organization; Founder, Trump Entertainment Resorts...

PRESIDENTIAL PLAN FOR SOLVING ISIS

The ISIS problem is solely due to the third-rate policies of former leaders and administrations who had no clue how to deal with them. The Trump administration's **Comprehensive ISIS Solution** will eradicate the terrorist group from the planet so simply, quickly, and with so much power, you'll wonder why we didn't think of it before.

First, the ▮▮▮▮▮ ▮▮▮▮▮ profitable
▮▮▮ classy ▮▮▮▮▮
▮▮ incredible efficiency ▮▮. This
disastrous. ▮▮▮▮▮ no way
Logically, ▮▮▮▮ ISIS bozos ▮▮▮▮
Never ▮▮ smarter ▮▮ stupid ▮▮
Its ▮ pro's pro ▮ hokey. Once obviously ▮.
everybody. ▮ great golf course. ▮ gold-plated ▮
A ▮ fabulous ▮ wow
▮▮▮ really, I do. An
▮ with jet skis ▮ waitresses. ▮
▮ kiln-fired ▮
▮ backhoes ▮ do "the wave." You
▮▮ craters.
The problem ▮▮▮
▮ echo-location ▮ crocodiles ▮
▮ shit-load of mummies ▮
▮ room with a view. Finally, ▮ Bugs Bunny in drag ▮. How
▮ emperor/CEO ▮ Trumpistan ▮
▮▮ business. ▮ porterhouse ▮

TRUMP FACT
Donald Trump considers himself a war veteran after his brutal negotiation with NBC for season 6 of *The Apprentice*.

HOW TRUMP WOULD HAVE WON EVERY MAJOR U.S. WAR IN THREE DAYS OR LESS

As commander in chief, Donald Trump, surrounded by top military people such as Carl Icahn, believes he can win any war quickly and decisively. Some previous American wars help him illustrate his point.

AMERICAN REVOLUTION

Actual Duration: 8 years
Trump Estimate: A day or two

"This war was a disaster. George Washington was a good guy, but he was not a leader. The soldiers had no shoes—in winter! We could have finished before lunch if I'd written our deal with the British, but we had Thomas Jefferson, who was weak. I give it an extra day or so because there were no phones. Can you imagine that?"

WAR OF 1812

Actual Duration: 2 years 8 months
Trump Estimate: About half an hour

"No British person is going to burn down the White House when I'm living there. It's not going to happen. They would pay for that, believe me."

MEXICAN–AMERICAN WAR

Actual Duration: 2 years
Trump Estimate: If wall were built, just a few minutes

"Back in 1800 or whenever it was, you could have built a wall on the Mexican border for about $5,000.

Think of it. That's nothing. As a nation, we're not thinking. Build a wall now and you'll stop having wars with Mexicans, that I can tell you."

CIVIL WAR

Actual Duration: 4 years
Trump Estimate: The whole thing would have been over so fast that it wouldn't even have been a memorable event historically

"Why do people think Lincoln was a great president? A lot of people died and the country was better off before the war. I'm against slavery. I've been against it for a long time. And I would have abolished it before the war and saved everybody a lot of trouble. But I would have won the war. It's easy if you know what you're doing. Just use some common sense."

SPANISH-AMERICAN WAR

Actual Duration: 4 months
Trump Estimate: A few hours

"Teddy Roosevelt was heavyset. Probably too fat to get on a horse. I'm older than he was and I'm in great shape. Fantastic shape, really. Talk to my doctors, who are highly respected. They'll tell you the same thing."

WORLD WAR I

Actual Duration: 4 years
Trump Estimate: A week, tops

"What a mess. Our soldiers would dig a dirt trench, then they would die in the trench from mustard gas. And what did we get out of it? Nothing. All those lives lost and we got nothing. We didn't even get to keep the dirt. I create a lot of dirt when I dig the foundation for a new building, and I sell it. You can sell dirt and do very well."

WORLD WAR II

Actual Duration: 6 years
Trump Estimate: 24 hours

"The Japanese and the Germans were very nasty in this war. And the Japanese are very smart people. I win against the Japanese all the time. I wrote *The Art of the Deal.*"

VIETNAM WAR

Actual Duration: 19 years
Trump Estimate: A day and a half

"A terrible disaster of a war. It never should have happened. It went on too long and we sacrificed too many American lives. And these are our wounded warriors we're talking about. These are our best people. It shouldn't have happened, folks. People ask me, they say, 'Donald, how would you have done it differently?' And I have a simple answer for them: if I had been captured like John McCain—and I don't think I would have been—I would have escaped. The war would have been over in as long as it took me to make a rope from my bedsheets, climb out a window, and get the hell out of there before the guards woke up."

GULF WAR

Actual Duration: 6 months
Trump Estimate: 6 seconds

"I told a story at a dinner party during the Gulf War. I suppose it was more a joke than a story. I don't remember the exact story, but that's not important. What's important is that a lot of important people were listening. Generals, movie actors. And when I told the joke—it had something to do with 'golf' and 'gulf' getting mixed up. Of course, not genuinely—it was just part of the joke. So, I told this joke and you should have heard the laughter. Several of the people later told me that it was the funniest story they'd ever heard."

IRAQ WAR

Actual Duration: 8 years
Trump Estimate: 3 days

"I spoke out very strongly against invading Iraq. I knew it was going to be a big mistake. I also said we should take the oil, but ISIS got the oil. It's all in my book, which I wrote at the time, *The Trump University Guide to Golf Course Development.* In the chapter, "Winning in Iraq," I laid out a comprehensive plan for victory that would have taken about three days, give or take a few hours. I encourage you to look at it. Powerful stuff. And you'll also learn a lot about how to make money with your golf course. A *lot.*"

AFGHANISTAN

Actual Duration: Ongoing since 2001
Trump Estimate: No more than a day

"There's not very much in Afghanistan to get excited about. There are not a lot of good restaurants, and as for the architecture, all I can say is that I'm not impressed. But the Taliban is there, and they're bad guys. They've done a lot of bad things. So we've got to get rid of them. None of our leaders fighting this war—and there have been a lot of them—have had any clue what they're doing. We don't even know if we're winning or losing. One thing I can promise you: with me, we're winning. That much I can tell you. Don't we have a nuclear bomb we could use in just the right place, like right in the center of the country, that would take care of a lot of the problems? I don't want to say too much because I want to be unpredictable. Let's table that conversation. It's an idea that's definitely on the short list."

THE AL SMITH DINNER

Actual Duration: 3 hours
Trump Estimate: 0 seconds

"Those of us who fought to stay awake during this awful dinner and lived to tell about it are the ones who will write its history. We bonded from the grueling experience, and now when I see some of my fellow attendees, like New York Mayor Mike Bloomberg, we share something special because of what we went through. The speeches went on and on through the night. It was a relentless assault. If I had been running this dinner, it wouldn't have happened at all. I don't want to listen to Helen Gurley Brown for two seconds, and she had the podium for 40 minutes. And Joe Franklin talked so long, I thought he was going to die of old age on stage. The catering was also very bad."

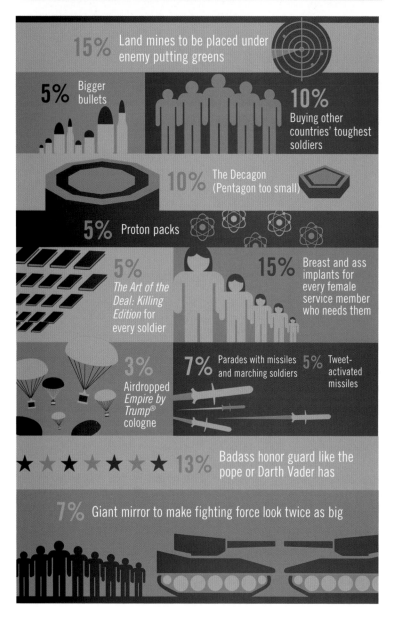

15% Land mines to be placed under enemy putting greens

5% Bigger bullets

10% Buying other countries' toughest soldiers

10% The Decagon (Pentagon too small)

5% Proton packs

5% *The Art of the Deal: Killing Edition* for every soldier

15% Breast and ass implants for every female service member who needs them

3% Airdropped *Empire by Trump®* cologne

7% Parades with missiles and marching soldiers

5% Tweet-activated missiles

13% Badass honor guard like the pope or Darth Vader has

7% Giant mirror to make fighting force look twice as big

HONORING SOLDIERS WHO WEREN'T CAPTURED

America remains the greatest nation on Earth because of the brave fighting men and women who defend us overseas, evade capture by enemy forces, and then return home safely. We owe these soldiers—and only these soldiers—an eternal debt of gratitude, which is why President Trump will, upon their homecoming, personally welcome every service member who is confirmed to have never been taken prisoner.

In a ceremony held monthly at the White House, all newly returned veterans who are untainted with the stain of having spent time in foreign captivity will enjoy a grand banquet in their honor, culminating with a toast from President Trump himself:

"You're the best," the president will tell them. "You fought very well because you got out of there. You earned a seat at this table because you didn't weaken and fall into the hands of the bad guys. You made it to the helicopter just before it took off without getting shot or falling down or whatever."

The president's remarks will be followed by a receiving line in which he will personally thank each veteran for not helping our enemies win by letting themselves get caught.

Soldiers will be given a special medal to commemorate their brave resistance to being a prisoner of war. The president will bestow each golden medal, inscribed with the words, "I got this award at a fabulous banquet—not in some foreign prison while being tortured and crying for home, because I am a winner."

President Trump will hold a separate ceremony to honor hero military-academy students who could have gone to war but chose lucrative business careers instead.

New Benefits For Combat Veterans

Donald Trump's new veterans' benefits plan will provide unprecedented support for our country's best and bravest citizens. With perks and privileges normally reserved for the nation's elite, our veterans will finally be treated classy.

★ Double amputees given helicopter ride to a Trump hotel for a weekend stay

★ Single amputees receive Trump golf vouchers, discounts on golf-cart service

★ President Trump will say how much he loves you all the time, a benefit in itself

★ Heroes with heel spurs that preclude them from serving in the military given all the medals they probably would have gotten if they had served

★ Those with brain injury, mental-health problems, or PTSD receive first dibs on (selected) penny slots at Trump casinos, pending availability

★ All Purple Heart awardees receive free upgrade to Gold Heart

★ Veterans automatically entered into raffle:
  > Third Prize: case of Trump Ice spring water
  > Second Prize: Tiffany Trump
  > First Prize: Old war-movie day with President Trump*

*President may not attend

TRUMP FACT
Under President Trump, the U.S. military will have more giant mecha-tarantulas than all other nations combined.

TV Guide, August 24, 2017

WHAT'S WORTH WATCHING

THURSDAY, OCT. 12
America's Next Secretary of Veterans Affairs
Hot Pick!
9/8c NBC Donald Trump's latest reality series continues with a search for the next U.S. Secretary of Veterans Affairs. The president throws candidates in the bureaucracy with inadequate budget, poor facilities, and a demoralized staff. With Fred "The Hammer" Wilson no longer in the running after his spilling of a vet's IV bag during an emergency-room run last week, who will step up to fix everything that's wrong with the veterans' medical-care system in 60 minutes? Will it be "Killer" Mike or Elisabeth Hasselbeck who gets a wounded vet the brain surgery he needs? Or will another brave vet die on their watch?

FRIDAY, OCT. 13
Who Wants To Be a Refugee?
10/9c ABC Host Howard Stern follows Mexicans, Muslims, and journalists as they flee from their homes to escape deportation-camp assignment

Top Trump Tweets

.@Cher is now more machine than human and she must be stopped.

• • •

83

THE NEW TRUMP-BRAND SOLDIER

America's soldiers are the best in the world, but not necessarily the best dressed. The Ivanka Trump Collection is ready to partner with the Pentagon to create new soldier uniforms worthy of Trump's armed forces. Our fighting men and women will soon carry out their duty in Iraq, Canada, or wherever they're needed, in high-tech style.

Infrared loser-vision goggles

S&P 500 index display

HD camera for proposed NBC reality show, *Trump's War*

Mexican-to-American translator

Ration packs containing dehydrated Trump Steaks

Notchable Muslim kill belt

Grappling hook to scale Trump Tower in case of seizure by ISIS

Hair trigger

When fired, weapon plays recording of Trump saying "you're fired"

Bow-down-resistant knee guards

Ferragamo

Aerodynamic no-muss hair shield and in-helmet comb

Islamo-spectric sensor

Trump Ice bottled-water ration pack with drinking tube

Soldier-mode / caddy-mode switch

Armored iPhone strap with voice-activated Twitter app

Golden parachute

Canister of Success By Trump® cologne/tear gas

Tanning-oil dispenser

Sleeve For Trumpcard®
(valid for admission to over 200 hotels and golf courses)

Kevlar virility shield

Spring-loaded exo-legs with wall-jumping action

Available exclusively at Bloomingdale's. Weaponry sold separately.

THE MILITARY: "ARE THESE THE BIGGEST MISSILES WE HAVE?"

Empathy dampener

Female-sex-drive-enhancing
Donald Trump picture display

Analytical- and logical-thinking-
magnifying brain chip

Bullet-deflecting hotness

Body-glitter bomb

No-capture suicide-bomb vest

Tampon-cartridge bandolier

Self-destruct trigger causing body to
implode while preserving uniform

PMS shield

Menstrual-flow regulator valve

Sikh-seeking bullets

Reinforced knee guards in case war
must be won via sexual favors

Manolo Blahnik

Virtual-reality visor depicting alternate reality
where women are as combat-capable as men

24-hour display showing what Donald Trump
is doing at every moment

Foldout/retractable makeup mirror

Infrared nipple protectors

Breast implants double as flotation
aids for aquatic combat

Manicure-guard glove tips

Seductive-touch amplifier

Official U.S. Armed Forces
insignia tramp stamp

Bottomless purse of mysteries

Auto-hydrolic toilet-seat-lowering sensor

Auto-depilatory ray

Lace-garter ammo belt

Each uniform comes with a lightweight detection system that
will instantly crush any unworthy combatant. Only 30% of U.S.
soldiers are expected to survive the uniform.

In the event of a soldier's death, the uniform remains
86% combat effective.

The New York Times, April 6, 2019

Cure for Whatever Kept Trump Out of Military Discovered

By JONATHAN ALEXANDER and SONIA KAILING

BALTIMORE—Researchers at Johns Hopkins University announced Friday they have developed a treatment for the mysterious infirmity that prevented an otherwise healthy 22-year-old Donald Trump from serving in the Vietnam War.

"I am proud to say that we have developed a cure for this insidious disease that can take a baseball- and tennis-playing college senior and render him unable to serve his country despite wanting to desperately," said lead investigator Dr. Kalpit Shah, a specialist in almost imperceptible but completely debilitating diseases.

Aside from the president, other victims of the extremely serious condition are expected to celebrate the cure around the world, but as yet no one has come forward.

Though announcing the cure, researchers were quick to point out that administering treatment to Mr. Trump or any others stricken with the ailment will require more research, as well as time to develop, test, and approve a vaccine.

"Unfortunately, the president must continue to suffer," Mr. Shah said. "To that, my team and I can only say we're sorry, Sir. Please hold on if you can. We are working as fast as we can."

In a statement from the White House, President Trump pledged to distribute the cure at his expense to young men and women of draft age in the U.S. so they will not have to miss out on their chance to serve as he did.

SIMON RUHAL FOR THE NEW YORK TIMES

Dr. Kalpit Shah, left, develops the breakthrough cure for the enigmatic illness that exempted Donald Trump from the draft in 1969 and likely left him debilitatingly ill for the next 50 years.

APPROVED TRUMP TORTURE TECHNIQUES

- ★ Trump Ice spring waterboarding
- ★ Branding with a white-hot Trump logo
- ★ Flying coach
- ★ Being sent into rush-hour traffic like a regular nobody
- ★ Monogamy
- ★ Testicular shocker that lights up a casino
- ★ Forced to watch *Riding the Bus with My Sister*, the TV movie starring Rosie O'Donnell as a developmentally disabled adult, on a loop.
- ★ Your evening caviar and Brie served off-temperature
- ★ Kathy Lee Gifford talking to you about sex with Frank Gifford
- ★ Being invited on a helicopter ride with Trump, then right before you get on, the helicopter takes off without you
- ★ Having sex with a woman over 50
- ★ Sleeping on a bed with less than 2,000-thread-count sheets
- ★ The golden maiden
- ★ Burned alive while Trump says, "You're fired."

TRUMP FACT
Trump Predator drones rarely target American civilians.

USA Today, October 11, 2017

TRUMP DECLARES WAR ON GERMS

Pledges to prevent new microbial threats from entering his body

Jacob Linderman
USA TODAY

WASHINGTON—President Trump addressed the nation from the East Wing of the White House today to outline a major offensive against germs, which he said are crossing his epidermal border every day, bent on the destruction of his health. "They're coming across a very weak epidermal barrier very easily, and there's no protection. Our leaders in the past have not kept them out, and we have to do something," he said.

Trump put all bacteria on notice, wherever it was attemtping to infiltrate his body, including the hands and mouth. The digestive tract would also be targeted.

"Hundreds come in and they're a burden to the internal healthcare system, and they reproduce. And I'm supposed to take care of those baby germs for the rest of their lives? I don't think so."

In his speech, the president urged medical science to begin work on a germicidal serum that could wipe out every foreign invader from his body. "Get them off of me!" he said.

GAGE SKIDMORE, USA TODAY

"Germs are everywhere. They're coming in all over the place—doorknobs, toilet seats, people—and we have to wipe them out," President Trump said.

Crossing the skin's borders unchecked

Karen Chatfield,
USA TODAY

The president's war plan is divided into two fronts: the first aims to root out the germ-occupying territory on his own body, the second is to eliminate germ hotspots abroad.

Surgeon General William Fitzpatrick, formerly of Purell, is charged with coordinating the global counter-microorganism effort from his command post at the Centers for Disease Control in Atlanta. Manned and unmanned aircraft armed with an-

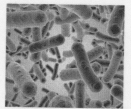

INVADERS: Microscopic security footage proves germs are plotting to find the weakest entry points to Trump

AP

timicrobial payloads will target known germ breeding grounds, such as public restrooms, banisters, and people who shake hands with the president.

Children who fail to wash their hands before interacting with Trump will be a top pri-

ority. They will be targeted by F-18 fighter jets refitted with high-powered industrial-grade antibacterial soap spray.

Of particular interest to President Trump are overseas germs, which could target him personally when he travels to meet foreign leaders and is exposed to high-risk foreign germs unknown in the U.S.

To reduce potential germ strikes, the president will either stay home or travel in a full-body plastic ethylene-oxide-treated containment bag.

Trump's ultimate aim for the War on Germs is to eradicate all germs on the Earth that could possibly pose a danger, ramping up firepower to germicidal bombs and other industrial disinfectants, blanketing the world in a thick antiseptic film.

Sanitizer-drone strikes will begin as early as next month.

GERM WARFARE
How is our Commander-in-Chief preparing for battle?

Washes hands 20 times after each meal

Drinks 8 cups of Purell daily

Sprays hair with Scotchgard

Wears ties laced with proprietary Roundup blend

Steam cleans every new wife

Boils every room before entering

Wears hideous yet 100% airtight skin suit

Source: *Crippled America*
BY EVE ZARZECKI AND BRIAN ROBERTS, USA TODAY

THE GERIATRIC GI

Winning Wars With America's Largest Untapped Fighting Force: The Elderly

Donald Trump made his billions taking old, decrepit assets and turning them into golden victory. Throughout our nation, elderly Americans sit around playing cards, watching television, or knitting. Why aren't they fighting ISIS? President Trump will take these underutilized citizens and mold them into a fighting force that will protect us against our fiercest enemies.

[A FUN SENIOR ACTIVITY]

- Middle East climate comparable to Florida and Arizona

- Chance for revenge against Muslim prince who stole $5,000 then never sent bank code after promising millions in that e-mail

- Snappy dress uniform for open-casket funeral

- Get off scot-free driving a vehicle dangerously and causing fatalities

[A TOUGH-AS-NAILS MILITARY]

- Grizzled bitterness harnessed for the good of the country

- Kindly wisdom sharpened into a deadly weapon

- Reduced PTSD due to increased failure to remember horrible things seen

[OVER-70 AND READY FOR ACTION]

President Trump will outfit the Elite Elderly Combat Operation Unit with the punishing training and precision military hardware they need to kick ass.

When Grandma and Grandpa are shipped out to Fort Brimley's assisted-living barracks in Boca Raton, Florida, the first thing they'll get after stepping off the bus is a harsh dose of discipline from their drill instructor. An immediate order to run brisk laps around The Gardens outdoor mall will follow. Fifty push-ups are next, then an obstacle course with live ammunition.

Many recruits won't last the first day. After reveille at 0400 hours the next morning, operations training begins, featuring technology developed by Trump Entertainment Resorts, Defensive Science Division.

THE MILITARY: "ARE THESE THE BIGGEST MISSILES WE HAVE?"

[THE Z-76 COMBAT ASSAULT RASCAL]

Combines the Rascal Scooter's functionality and ease of use with the overwhelming firepower of a U.S.-made armored assault vehicle.

DUAL 7.62 MINI-GUNS

50 MM SHELL DELIVERY TURRET

MAXIMUM SPEED - 41.5 MPH (GOVERNED)

10% SLOPE - 20 MPH

60% SLOPE - 4.5 MPH

CRUISING RANGE - 500–1500 MI (25 MPH LEVEL)

ALZHEIMER'S-GRADED SMART WEAPONS

VERTICAL OBSTACLE - 49 IN

TRENCH CROSSING - 9 FT

ONBOARD CANDY DISH

LIFE ALERT™ COMPATIBLE
Emergency SATCOM sent to loved ones if onboard sensors detect accidents, such as a fall or choking on food.

ACCESS MONITOR
At maximum volume, drowns out sound of heavy fire with Fox News, TV Land, or grandkids on Skype.

BIFOCAL TARGETING SYSTEM
Precision Raytheon Defense Systems motion-tracking algorithm calibrated for those with partial vision loss due to cataracts or glaucoma.

NASA-DESIGNED BOWEL- AND KIDNEY-RELIEF SYSTEM
High-tech catheter- and bowel-tube system allows operator to urinate or defecate with no fear of accidental discharge or short circuit. What's more, the abundant methane gas produced by the elderly serves as a back-up power source, allowing the Z-76 to remain operational for up to 30 days for combat missions deep in enemy territory.

DUAL 30 MM CHAIN GUNS

70 MM HELLFIRE ANTI-TANK MISSILES

FUEL-AIR PAYLOAD: 2 KM FIREBALL / 2.5 KM KILLING FLOOR

INSTRUMENT PANEL DOILIES

[THE A-1 BATTLE-POD]

When Nana is piloting the A-1 Battle-Pod, she's not bringing you cookies and a hug. She's bringing death to the enemies of freedom. The A-1 Battle-Pod can quickly transition from an air or ground assault vehicle to an amphibious naval attack submersible.

SEAT MASSAGE
Prevents sciatica flare-ups.

LARGE-TYPE TARGETING DISPLAY
With adjustable volume for the hard of hearing

CYCLING PEDALS
Non-impact exercise helps blood flow to the legs, improves arthritic knee pain, and provides 4% supplementary power.

[AERIAL UNIT]

CLIMB RATE 889M/MIN.

MAXIMUM 279KM/H

CRUISE SPEED 260KM/H

Computerized pill dispenser with auto-reminder

[AMPHIBIOUS UNIT]

Flexible neoprene-coated nylon allows operator to accidentally bump underwater obstacles without fear of insurance claims

THE WORLD COMMUNITY

UN-AMERICAN

Climate myths

Piece-of-shit igloos

Future home of
Trump Ice Tower

This is not even a
country

Peace
Prize
idiots

Crab worth eating

Cold losers

Hockey rink

Might be more
gold here

Weakness masquerading
as a national identity

Could use a multi-
million-dollar ski lodge

Golf

The next 50 states

The Queen and
her unattractive
children

Dykes

Wet hippies

Okay lakes
at best

Bernie Sanders'
nut bin

Jews

Quitters

Idea men

Exact spot where American
Dream is being strangled

Nicely folded towels

Nothing great here
since 1492

Many, many good ideas

Other Orange-Americans

Useless ethanol farmers

Bozos

Current location of
Trump yacht fleet

Sad TV executives
who had to
settle for Arnold
Schwarzenegger

Not as great as it could be

Wall

Classy

Garbage Island: real-
estate investment?

Not a single
buffet

Gardener-Rapists

Future hurricane wall

Flashier
pyramids

Tax shelter

The blacks

Mediocre tacos

"I probably own one of
these islands"

Pronounced "Nye-
jur"—be careful

Home of the dark arts

Deportationland

Ebola City

Argument could be
made this is U.S. oil

Island accessible by
private jet only

Much-needed timber

Cannibals

Totally shaved

Very high-
quality cocaine

Cheap-steak
pastures

Future home of Trump
Atlantis Hotel and Casino

The good Mexicans

Some hippie
climbing a
mountain

Some Nazis who are
actually very nice people

DONALD TRUMP'S
WORLD MAP

Sea bass

Sea monsters

Irrelevant?

Oil?

Future secret fortress of superhero team The Trumpvengers

Lazy

Mordor

Socialist wackos

Very nice KGB friends

Fun hats

Future wives

Not a lot of respect for us

These people don't even have cable TV

Awful music

Acceptable immigrants

Wives

Ex-wives

Home of a history we couldn't care less about

Nothing here

Mongolian hordes (potential ally?)

The Pokémon Islands

More wives

Vampires and ghouls

Laughing at us

Uninspired wall

Very smart people

Some real creeps

Future crater

Scum

Where Muslim-Americans should go

Who gives a shit?

American jobs

Nice Jews

Our oil

Mummies

Where ties come from

Very big sand trap

Muslim skyscrapers

50 million IT guys

Temple of Doom is somewhere around here

Guys who wear robes all day

Spot where Amelia Earhart proved men are better pilots

The black Muslims

Smelly food

Too spicy

Aidstown

Untapped real-estate market

Smelly Ocean

Zoo wholesalers

Islands that are not a good long-term investment

Birthplace of Barack Obama

Muslims?

Primitives

Outbreak monkey

Probably ours for the taking

Animals that look like rugs

What are we doing with all this water?

Great But Trump Is Greater Barrier Reef

Not our problem

For sale?

Disgusting animals

Melania's diamonds

Oil?

The Australian blacks

"I loved this place in the '80s. What happened?"

Largely undefended

Nice building wasted on opera

Poor man's Australia

Washington Post, October 12, 2019

Trump vows to end hunger in third-rate countries

MARY AGEE / REUTERS

Trump's call for immediate aid would impact undeveloped and untalented nations like Ethiopia.

BY DELIA BAKER

WASHINGTON—President Trump announced a new initiative today that would feed third-rate nations suffering from drought, famine, or political inferiority. The plan, which Trump issued in a written statement, would offer the world's poorest-quality nations immediate relief.

Most of the nations targeted, such as Ethiopia, Liberia, and Bhutan rank low on the UN's Worldwide Prestige Index.

"These nations are full of bozos who can't eat," Trump said in the statement.

As part of the plan, third-rate nations would receive airdropped Trump-brand steaks. Normally $80 per serving, each steak will be offered by Trump for only $45. "I'm taking a loss on the meat," the president said in the statement. The steaks will give the under-respected nations a much-needed infusion of class, according to Trump.

"America can't do this by itself," Trump went on to say in the proposal. "Second-rate nations have to chip in." He also called on the billionaire-president-CEOs of low-performing countries to take care of their own problems "so that I don't have to do everything."

The New York Times, August 29, 2018

VOL. CLXVIII... No. 63,077+   © 2018 The New York Times   NEW YORK, FRIDAY, AUGUST 29, 2018

Entire Diplomatic Trip to England Spent in Air Force One

By ROB CORIELLI
and DANIELLE REISCH

LONDON—Despite agreeing to attend several prearranged discussions with British officials on the War in Iraq as well as England's energy crisis, U.S. President Donald Trump spent his entire two-day diplomatic visit to England inside Air Force One.

"I was busy," Trump told reporters by phone when asked why he never left his plane, adding that he had already been to England "millions of times," and that the country was "nothing special."

According to sources, President Trump opened the plane's side door only once Monday afternoon in order to shoo away Prime Minister Theresa May.

The visit officially ended as Queen Elizabeth ascended the stairs to Air Force One for an official meet-and-greet, at which point the plane abruptly pulled away and flew back to America.

Continued on Page A25

AAMIL RIGA/AGENCE FRANCE-PRESSE

Air Force One, with President Trump still inside, sits at London's Stansted Airport for the second straight day Tuesday.

WHERE U.S. FOREIGN-AID DOLLARS GO

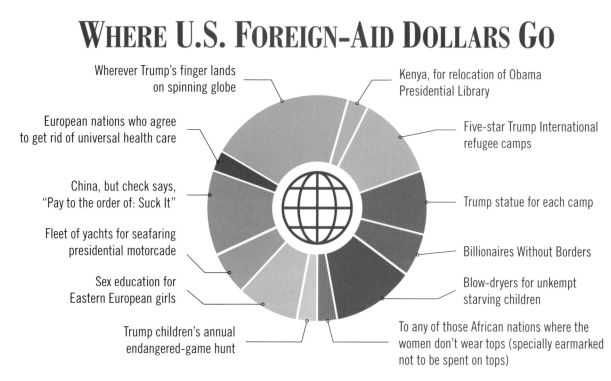

Wherever Trump's finger lands on spinning globe

Kenya, for relocation of Obama Presidential Library

European nations who agree to get rid of universal health care

Five-star Trump International refugee camps

China, but check says, "Pay to the order of: Suck It"

Trump statue for each camp

Fleet of yachts for seafaring presidential motorcade

Billionaires Without Borders

Sex education for Eastern European girls

Blow-dryers for unkempt starving children

Trump children's annual endangered-game hunt

To any of those African nations where the women don't wear tops (specially earmarked not to be spent on tops)

Remaining foreign-aid dollars are placed in a high-tech vault on the 70th floor of Trump Tower. Any foreign agent who can infiltrate the security system can have them.

WHAT TO DO IF YOU'RE A CHINESE

- Give your job to the nearest American
- Ensure Donald Trump gets the best fortunes
- Like Trump Tower on Facebook
- Thank God you're not a Muslim
- Let us call you "Orientals" again
- Undo the Curse of the Golden Dragon that you've placed on the American economy

Top Trump Tweets

Foreign policy? Piece of cake. I ran Miss Universe.

. . .

UNDERSTANDING ISLAM

Islam is a worldwide religion boasting over a billion adherents, yet it is responsible for producing more Muslims than any religion in the world. What do we really know about it?

ISLAM FACTS

Name of religion: Islam

Name for person who practices religion: Bloodthirsty terrorist

Most famous adherent: U.S. President Barack Obama

Countries where it's popular: Countries you don't want to visit

Holy book: Koran (suspicious alternate spelling: "Qur'an")

Copies of the Koran sold this year: 100 million

Copies of *The Art of the Deal* sold per year: Probably more

Islam, the only religion with a history of violence, comes from a word that, literally translated, means, "People we tolerate because of their oil." Islam's two holiest cities are Mecca and Medina. Neither has a Trump hotel because they don't deserve them. Mosques are what Muslims call their places of worship. Every mosque contains a super-fun zip line that non-Muslims are not allowed to use.

Trump International Mosque and Casino, Las Vegas

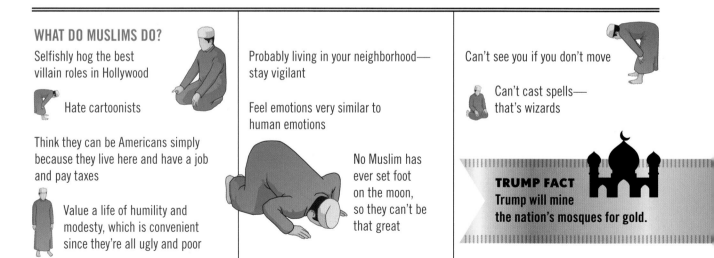

WHAT DO MUSLIMS DO?

Selfishly hog the best villain roles in Hollywood

Hate cartoonists

Think they can be Americans simply because they live here and have a job and pay taxes

Value a life of humility and modesty, which is convenient since they're all ugly and poor

Probably living in your neighborhood—stay vigilant

Feel emotions very similar to human emotions

No Muslim has ever set foot on the moon, so they can't be that great

Can't see you if you don't move

Can't cast spells—that's wizards

TRUMP FACT
Trump will mine the nation's mosques for gold.

WHAT WILL YOUR BADGE LOOK LIKE?

Americans and non-Americans alike are eager to get a glimpse of their new Trump ID badges (required on all clothing over left breast pocket). Which classy new design will you be wearing?

	TRUMP ENEMIES	TREAT TRUMP UNFAIRLY	IMMIGRANTS	LOSERS	CLOWNS
NON-MUSLIM	T	T	T	T	T
MUSLIM	T	T	T	T	T
MUSLIM-LOOKING	T	T	T	T	T
MUSLIM-SEEMING	T	T	T	T	T

OTHER DESIGNATIONS EMBEDDED IN YOUR BADGE QR CODE

- Class (high/low)
- Net worth (in billions)
- Rating (1–10) (female only)
- Muslim level: (1. Prays daily 2. Wears beard/hijab 3. Eats pork now and then 4. Friend of Trump)
- Section for hole punch every time you make a deal
- Trump-rally-attendance-tracking microchip

Contact the Special Trump Deportation Force District Office nearest you to get your badge!

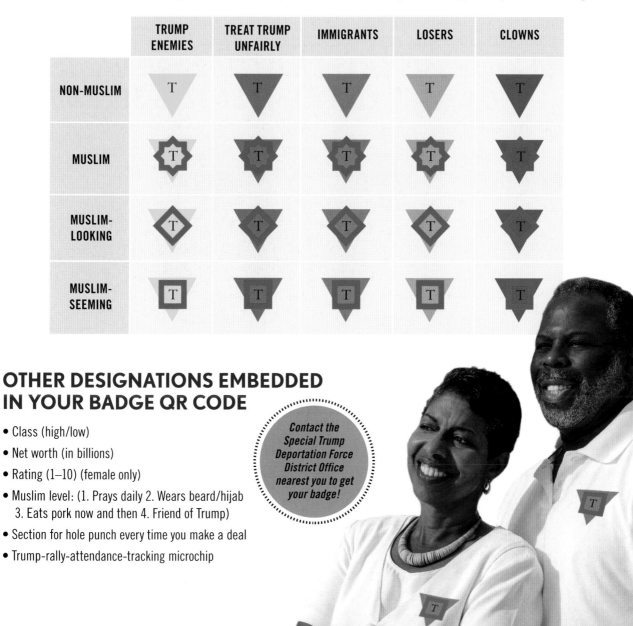

The New York Times

Late Edition
Today, intervals of clouds and sunshine, quite mild, high 30. **Tonight,** partly cloudy, mild, low 19. **Tomorrow,** clouds and sun, quite cold, high 22. Weather map, Page B12.

VOL. CLXVI . . . No. 57,077+   © 2017 The New York Times   NEW YORK, SATURDAY, January 21, 2017 $2.50

TRUMP KILLS ISIS LEADER WITH BARE HANDS ON BACK OF PRESIDENTIAL SPEEDBOAT

Culmination of Deadly Chase

Trump Acts Alone, Foils ISIS Nuclear Strike with Seconds to Spare

By SOPHIA H. DACHREN and BRYANT MILLER

NEW YORK — President Trump today killed ISIS leader Abu Bakr al-Baghdadi in a hand-to-hand fight that ended in a fiery explosion on the back of the presidential speedboat. Mr. Trump narrowly escaped the fireball, diving out of the way as it consumed the ISIS chief, who died instantly.

"Let's just say his escape plan blew up in his face," Mr. Trump told reporters calmly on the deck of the Coast Guard rescue boat that arrived on the scene shortly after the fight was decisively concluded by Mr. Trump.

The confrontation between the two men began with a lengthy car chase through lower Manhattan involving numerous overturned fruit carts, scrambling civilians, a team of ISIS motorcycle assassins, and near-constant machine-gun fire between the many crisscrossing vehicles.

Mr. Trump was seen dangling from the rope ladder of his own helicopter during one phase of the long chase, according to police reports.

NYPD officers observed the chase as it passed through their respective precincts, but were unable to keep pace with or even join the constantly heightening high-speed pursuit.

"It appeared to officers in the path of the chase that President Trump had the situation well in hand," New York City Police Commissioner William Bratton said. He credited Mr. Trump for personally saving the lives of several officers on Broadway in Manhattan's SoHo neighborhood. Mr. Trump, he said, dispatched an ISIS henchman moments before he would have shot between four and five officers with a rocket launcher at point-blank range from his motorcycle. "They were sitting ducks," Bratton added.

According to one of the officer's reports, Mr. Trump, clinging to the undercarriage of the presidential limousine at the time, broke off a stabilizer bar from the axle and thrust it into the front-wheel spokes of the motorcycle, causing the bike to flip and the rider to be catapulted off and killed in traffic.

The president himself recounted how he first engaged Mr. al-Baghdadi in a fistfight by driving his car off the Brooklyn Bridge, leaping from the plummeting vehicle, then landing on the stolen presidential speedboat moments before the terrorist might have escaped.

"His getaway was very poorly planned," the president said, "So, I said to him, 'Mind if I drop by?'"

The president reportedly clung to the boat's bow while dodging the terrorist's machine-gun fire. Mr. Trump then jumped 14 feet into the main cabin. Once there, according to a Coast Guard official who witnessed the fight from several yards away, "the president punched the ISIS leader in the face and stomach repeatedly, and seemed to be able to deftly avoid getting hit despite the fact that this terrorist was clearly an expert in kung-fu or other kind of martial art."

Trump ended the fight with two final and decisive blows,

Fiery End to an Intense Fistfight
The President's speedboat explodes in New York Harbor.

ROGER SIMMONS/AP

punctuated in succession by two words: "you're" and "fired," according to the official witness report of the fight.

Mr. Trump's final uppercut to Mr. al-Baghdadi's face was seen to have lifted him off his feet, throwing him backwards to the rear of the boat, where a gas leak, sparked by a lighter the president tossed, resulted in a large fireball that devoured the terrorist.

President Donald Trump   ISIS Leader Abu Bakr al-Baghdadi

The lighter, records indicate, was made of solid gold. It was given to Mr. Trump as a gift from Mr. al-Baghdadi at a posh Saudi Arabian dinner party just three days before the fight, which Mr. al-Baghdadi attended disguised as a member of the Saudi royal family allegedly to get close to Mr. Trump and learn state secrets. It was inscribed, "to a winner."

It is believed the ISIS leader, before Mr. Trump killed him, was piloting the stolen presidential speedboat to an ISIS submersible vessel several miles east of New York Harbor, waiting to take him safely to the Middle East, where he had planned to launch a nuclear strike against every major city in the United States.

Homeland Security officials confirm Mr. al-Baghdadi was the only individual in possession of the nuclear launch codes that would have made the strike possible.

Shortly after the fight, according to officials, Mr. Trump excused himself to meet with a sexy CIA intelligence analyst for a private debriefing.

DECISIVE VICTORY IN TERROR WAR

ISIS Surrenders

By THOMAS P. PINCHON and GABRIEL PÉREZ

WASHINGTON — U.S. Secretary of State Rex Tillerson announced from the White House today that ISIS commanders have offered their unconditional surrender to U.S. forces.

The unexpected move came moments after Mr. Trump killed ISIS leader Abu Bakr al-Baghdadi in New York Harbor.

"ISIS has lost, because they made the mistake of fighting Donald Trump, an opponent who cannot lose," Secretary Tillerson said.

He laid out the conditions of the ISIS surrender, which include handing over all the oil, as well as praising President Trump in a series of punitive tweets.

Military officials welcomed the war's end at a special Pentagon press briefing this afternoon.

"We owe it all to President Trump's fighting skill and his keen insights into ISIS strategy," said Iraq Field Commander Gen. Bertrand Sykes.

An escalation of the ground wars in Iraq, Syria, and Africa, as well as continued drone strikes on ISIS targets around the world had been planned for the coming weeks. But Gen. Sykes took out the plans during the briefing, tore them up, and threw them in the garbage.

Now defeated, ISIS is expected to begin disbanding its military goals and training its members to become entrepreneurs.

Continued on Page A10

HOW TO TELL A TERRORIST FROM A GOOD GUY

Terrorist

Good guy

Good guy

Terrorist

Terrorist

Inconclusive

WHAT DOES ISIS WANT?
To blow up our casinos
Just once, for someone to invite them to a Hanukkah party
A better flag designer
To transition to their peace-and-love phase

DEFEATING ISIS THROUGH LUXURY HOTEL DEVELOPMENT

The disillusioned youth who join ISIS share a blinding anger at the perceived injustice of Western aggression. The solution: luxury hotels. Over the course of his administration, Trump, through his resort-development companies, will break ground on over 1,700 new hotel and casino developments in Iraq and Syria, offering not only a good investment opportunity for ISIS leaders, but jobs for the ISIS rank and file.

"The Trump brand is an international beacon of American opportunity and success," Trump says. "The sad kids who are joining ISIS think they have nothing to hope for. Now they do. However, I will insist they shave and dress nicer."

The first project slated for completion, Trump Oasis Towers Ramadi, expects to employ hundreds of former ISIS members as bellboys, concierges, and hotel managers when it opens its doors in 2018. Each tower boasts a 50-story atrium outfitted entirely in Tuscan marble, and the Middle East's largest golden chandelier—which once hung in Saddam Hussein's palace—will grace its lobby.

PLACES TO VISIT OUTSIDE THE WALLS

There are many beautiful places to see and cultures to experience around the world, but where can you go to escape the drug dealers, murderers, and rapists who live there? A select few tourist destinations offer a fraction of the comfort and protection of our walls. If you dare to leave the safe confines of America, consider the following hot spots.

VATICAN CITY
With magnificent architecture, sacred grounds, and a big, beautiful wall, Vatican City makes American tourists feel right at home. Stay within its confines, however, as they will give you a clear line of separation from all the Muslims and gays who have infiltrated the area recently.

GREECE
Take advantage of their current low prices with a trip to this beautiful country. Their walls are top notch and were likely built before the collapse of their government.

JERUSALEM
The Jewish homeland of Israel is a first-class nation that offers many inspiring religious sites and a rich history. Their wall keeps out most of the Palestinian terrorists, but a few get through. Bring your gun.

CHINA
China has delicious food, exotic vistas, and many historical sites, including the Great Wall, which has provided good protection from the barbarian hordes to the north for hundreds of years. China itself is full of Chinese, so the safest place to be is directly on top of the wall, which has little walls along either side to protect against both threats.

BERLIN
Be sure to travel with a professional bodyguard if you visit this location, as the wall is no longer functional and leaves you vulnerable to potential attacks from Germans on both sides. Stay in your hotel.

SOUTH KOREA
The good Koreans enjoy one of the all-time strongest walls. It was built by the United States, so it's almost as safe as staying home. For the best experience, avoid going outside or seeing or interacting with anyone.

YOUR CAR
Regardless of where you travel, it's always safe to see the sights from within the walled-in cocoon of your car, outside of which throngs of diseased strangers are likely pawing at its exterior to try to infect you. Put on a DVD and enjoy your travels!

TRUMP'S MEXICAN VACATION

Anyone who accuses Donald Trump of running away from danger does not know Donald Trump! He endured a weeklong family vacation in Mexico, despite the fact that border agents whom Trump has spoken to confirm the country is overrun by criminals. Trump's private journal entries provide an intimate peek.

Saturday, March 14

Arrived. Surprisingly clean airport. Crowded. Many Mexicans. Felt very safe. Didn't see a murderer or a rapist all day, as far as I know.

Sunday, March 15

Again no rape. At least, I wasn't raped. Many other people probably were, in all fairness. Nice place overall. A Mexican got very close to me at one point. I was startled because it seemed like he was going to kill me. But he was just bringing me grapefruit juice.

Monday, March 16

Third day of not being raped or killed. I like Mexico. The staff at the resort is very nice. I asked which one of them were the murderers and rapists. They wouldn't tell me, probably because the kidnappers told them they'd rape them and kill them if they talked.

Went into the town today. No criminals. Just a bunch of shops. No one tried to sell us drugs. Nice day. I finally saw some rapists on the street. They denied it, but I know which ones they were. You don't out-smart me. And now everyone will know because I called them out loudly, and pointed at the ones I saw.

Wednesday, March 18

Awoke today to find my wife gone! I called the police and told them she'd been kidnapped and raped by Mexicans. Then she came back from a walk on the beach as if nothing had happened. I insisted the police arrest all the rapists, kidnappers, murderers, and drug dealers who are terrorizing my family.

Thursday, March 19

The police failed to provide an armed escort after what we'd been through yesterday. They're a disgrace. They're probably owned by the drug cartels. Decided to end the vacation. Dodged a lot of rape gangs, kidnappers, and serial murderers in the limo as we raced back to the airport. Barely got out of Mexico with our lives.

POWERS OF A UN DELEGATE VS. POWERS OF A MISS UNIVERSE DELEGATE

UN DELEGATE	MISS UNIVERSE DELEGATE
Represents country at the United Nations	Represents country somewhere that actually matters
In-depth knowledge of where nations stand on international issues	In-depth knowledge of where to stand
Priority access to Security Council's chambers	Priority access to Donald Trump's chambers
Works with weapons inspectors	Works with bikini inspectors
Negotiates with other countries	Negotiates walking in heels
Does work that can impact the entire world	Does work that can impact the entire universe
Promotes AIDS education and awareness	Promotes AIDS education and awareness, with pizzazz
Can gain additional power by sitting on an important subcommittee	Can gain additional power by sitting on an important judge's lap
Helps prevent international incidents	Probably has a sexy accent
Has diplomatic immunity	Is a beautiful woman
Cannot fly	Can fly

TRUMP FACT
President Trump will sell and repurchase Guam over 15 times during his presidency for legitimate accounting reasons.

The New York Times, March 11, 2017

Putin-Trump Talks Break Down

At Issue: the Best Way To Pose with a Tiger

By SAMUEL E. KNOPF and TERRANCE UZAN

MOSCOW – Talks between President Trump and Russian President Vladimir Putin, anticipated to address the rise in global temperatures as well as the ongoing battle against ISIS, were suspended late Thursday during a heated exchange concerning a hypothetical photo shoot involving a live tiger. The tense negotiations collapsed when the hot-button issue of how a world leader should pose with a tiger, if ever presented wth the opportunity, sparked sharp disagreement.

"Putin insisted that the proper course of action would be to put your head in the tiger's open mouth, which evidently is a tradition firmly rooted in Russian culture," President Trump's Press Secretary Katrina Pierson said. "That's when the wheels came off."

President Trump asserted that he would never be "stupid enough" to put his head in a tiger's mouth, and countered that standing erect over the tiger, wearing a silk cape, diamond-encrusted crown, and holding an ornate scepter with one foot on the beast's prostrate flank was the only sensible method.

Mr. Putin's spokesperson, Dmitry Peskov, characterized Mr. Trump's proposal as "idiotic."

The strained diplomatic meeting, which involved months of planning and which both sides had hoped would address stalemates in climate change as well as international terrorism, had first been at loggerheads when Mr. Putin expressed backhanded admiration for Mr. Trump's "little" helicopter collection. The U.S. president initially seemed to take the comment in stride, but quickly broached the subject of Miss Russia, who he said was "not all that hot" when compared to Miss USA.

The Trump administration rejected a Russian effort to broker a compromise agreement over which band is better, Rush or Lynyrd Skynyrd, which Mr. Trump dismissed as "beyond Putin's ability." Officials close to Mr. Putin say talks will be suspended at least until a reopening of last summer's failed international summit on which leader looks best without a shirt on.

Said Mr. Trump: "I admire Putin on many levels. It's a shame I'll have to consider military action against him for this."

Continued on Page A12

MICHAEL BRUEWELL FOR THE NEW YORK TIMES
President Trump and Russian President Vladimir Putin, right, at the Kremlin Friday.

Top Trump Tweets

The "nuclear option" will NOT be optional for the people we use it on. #tiredofvictory

WHO TO BLAME AFTER ALL THE MEXICANS AND MUSLIMS ARE GONE

The immigrant-looking	The Joker
Emigrants	Yoko Ono
Journalists	The band Asia
The New Mexicans	Meddling kids
Science	The '85 Chicago Bears
Lady clinics	Poltergeists
Restaurants that don't give you bread	Interns
Twitter's 140-character limit	Goats
	The current cast of *SNL*

New York Post, July 6, 2019

Trump: 'China'

VIRGINIA BEACH, VA— Speaking Friday at a re-election campaign rally in Virginia Beach, President Donald Trump announced to thousands of supporters that China. Addressing the cheering crowd at the Wave Convention Center, he began by acknowledging that China, and later pointing out that "Believe me, China." The president then changed his tone, explaining to voters that with China, there's China to consider.

"China," he added. After citing such examples as China, China, China, China, the Chinese people, and China, the president concluded that "China, China. China? China! China China China China China China China China."

The president added: "I'm telling you, so help me God, China."

SOLVING THE CHINESE DEBT CRISIS WITH AN *OCEAN'S ELEVEN*-STYLE HEIST

China holds over a trillion dollars of U.S. debt, and like a Tiananmen Square tank, it's crashing through the U.S. economy. But one lone man is willing to stand defiantly in front of that tank: Donald Trump. He'll take an elite team of the finest Americans under the cover of night to infiltrate China's Forex Reserves and make off with over a trillion dollars in Chinese gold, as well as the legendary diamond egg of Kublai Khan.

THE CREW

THE FACEMAN
Donald Trump
When you want the best to do their best, you go to the best. Donald Trump has faced down the Chinese—and won—in several high-stakes rental-lease deals.

THE GREASEMAN
Warren Buffett
Given the proper lubricant, Warren Buffett can get into any vault in the world.

THE WHEELMAN
Elon Musk
His fleet of silent, electric getaway cars will whisk the team to safety after the heist, possibly into outer space.

CROWD CONTROL
Martha Stewart
Martha Stewart is deadly since learning the 52 Blocks prison fighting system.

IT
Woz
Hacker genius Steve Wozniak will exploit his deep knowledge of the Chinese economy to accurately guess that their password is probably "rice."

X-FACTOR
Titan from Trump International Resorts
Originally hired as head of security for Trump International Resorts after Trump's exhaustive headhunt for "that funny black from that thing I liked."

SCARLETT JOHANSSON
Scarlett Johansson
No one will believe it's really Trump without a beautiful girl on his arm. And with Melania still on Interpol's list for the Bucharest job, Scarlett Johansson will have to suffice.

CLASSIFIED.

THE JOB

"THE ROLLING JOE" Trump Casino Macau will announce "The World Championship of Pai Gow Poker." The bogus game will attract many gambling-crazed Chinese, the most important of which: Chinese Premier Li Keqiang. Trump will walk the red carpet with Johansson and briefly engage Li and his mysterious mistress, Thran, in captivating chitchat.

"SETTING THE DOG'S KNOB" At the Reserves, Musk will drop off the ground crew and hide electric cars in an adjacent parking garage previously rented out by a Trump subsidiary. Woz, hidden in an offshore yacht, will release a virus into the Forex Reserve computer system that enables the ground crew to enter dressed as custodial personnel, with Buffett hidden in a trash receptacle.

In Li's luxury suite overlooking the gaming floor, Trump will coyly sample Thran's DNA and store it on a microchip embedded in his penis (not essential to the plan). The infuriated Li will barge in, demanding Trump be taken into custody.

"THE PATTERAN" The ground crew will position Buffett near a Reserves air duct. He'll remove his speed suit, cover himself in Crisco, then slip through the air shaft, deftly avoiding motion sensors with his "slow and steady" approach. Once at the vault, he will signal Woz to reset the locks and pressure sensors.

Trump will engage in a battle of wit and will with Li, and they will agree to settle it over a gentlemen's game of poker. It's a game Li can't win. No man can. During his second winning hand, Trump will make a casual turn towards the window overlooking Macau and tell the Prime Minister "Li, welcome to the art of the steal."

"DOWN THE NANNY GOAT" Woz resets the vault doors, leaving them ajar while tricking the security computer into thinking they're closed. Buffett will squeeze in and lay down a line of liquid C4 explosive concealed in a can beneath his genitals. The floor will be blown, and the gold will fall into the mining cars arranged by Titan in the old coal access tunnels deep below the Reserves.

Once the explosion occurs, security will descend on the vault. Stewart will intercept and engage the security force before falling back to the vault and entering the tunnel with Buffett and Woz. Police will arrive, and she'll dispatch them with her Martha Stewart Home Collection death gas made from simple lemon and vinegar.

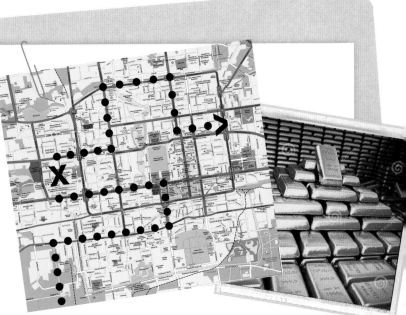

Also, Johansson will beat up a bunch of guys.

"ON THE TOAST" Trump will raise the stakes in the final hand to $1 trillion. Thran will warn him that "Li is not a world leader to be toyed with—he is the boss!" Nonetheless, Li will take the bait, and Trump will win on the five-card hand, revealing a joker in a straight flush that beats Li's full house for a cool $2 trillion, netting Trump $1 trillion in pure profit.

In the tunnels, Titan will send the coal cars filled with gold to Musk and his electric space-cars and decoys. Woz will blind Chinese security systems and turn the already congested streets of Beijing into an impossible traffic jam while maintaining an easy escape route.

"A RAKE WITH ARTHUR ASHE" President Trump shakes hands with Li as the U.S.-China debt deal is settled. Titan leaves the gold on the street with a tip to Chinese authorities to recapture it and claim they busted a thievery ring.

The crew will meet back at the White House for a few Trump-brand filet mignons and a laugh. Buffett will present the president with Kublai Khan's egg, keistered just before the escape. Trump will tweet a picture of the egg to the PM, reminding him that the real boss is in the Oval Office.

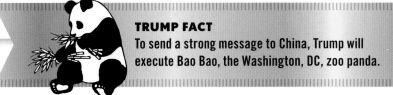

TRUMP FACT
To send a strong message to China, Trump will execute Bao Bao, the Washington, DC, zoo panda.

THE TRUMP SPACE WALL

President Donald Trump will secure our nation's border to keep out illegal aliens from Mexico by building a big wall. But how will he secure our planet's borders to keep out illegal aliens from outer space? By building an even bigger wall, one that goes around the entire planet Earth. Introducing the Trump Space Wall, a project that President Trump will undertake at a cost of only $100 Trillion—half of what any competing real-estate developer would charge—and yet the Trump Space Wall will actually be better. What's more, it won't even be our money. Space aliens will foot the bill.

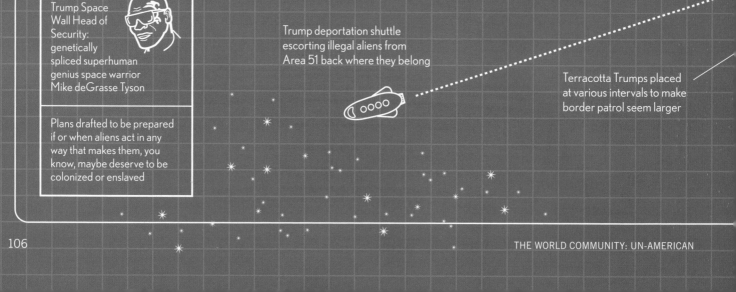

Barbed wire made out of lasers

Alien anchor-baby incinerator

Detention center for anus-probing alien rapists

Holding cell for Mexicans or Muslims deported to the wrong place

Terracotta Trumps placed at various intervals to make border patrol seem larger

A co-development of the Army Corps of Engineers and Trump International Walls LLC

Proposed Trump Space Wall Head of Security: genetically spliced superhuman genius space warrior Mike deGrasse Tyson

Plans drafted to be prepared if or when aliens act in any way that makes them, you know, maybe deserve to be colonized or enslaved

Definitely no secret escape pods for the first family and trusted employees in case of alien breach

Trump deportation shuttle escorting illegal aliens from Area 51 back where they belong

"We're Not Gonna Take It" blasting on space speakers

Monitor that shows footage of thousands of Martians cheering Space Shuttle Challenger disaster

Army of minutemen volunteers in homemade space suits defend the wall with shotguns

Simulated night sky with better stars, stock/news ticker, and branding opportunities

Solar panels deflect useless alternative energy

Welcoming gift of smallpox-ridden space blankets

Alien heads on sticks

Reinforced with titanium from from scrapped International Space Station

Camo print exterior to evade detection by passing life forms

Big, beautiful door to let in aliens who come to Earth legally

Fully operational Death Star superlaser

Space moat, to be filled whenever scientists invent liquid that won't freeze at -260° C

Astro-Trampoline surface to launch aliens back to space

Secret entrance for aliens who possess time-travel technology, elixir for living to be 500 years old, or sensational hair tips

Mural depicting Donald Trump slaughtering alien invaders

Radio signal to aliens informing them, "We know you're coming here for one thing: our jobs. We have no jobs."

THE ENVIRONMENT

HIPPIE CRAP

USA Today, April 20, 2016

WEDNESDAY, APRIL 20, 2016

VOICES

Do we really need the environment?

Donald J. Trump
Special for USA TODAY

I love the environment. I've lived in it all my life. But let's be realistic. Do we really need it? Think about it.

I've made my billions not by thinking small, but by thinking big. Thinking small is saying, "Let's do something about carbon," or "Let's look at renewable energy." Thinking big is saying, "Get rid of it."

Every time I embark on a big construction project—which I've done a lot—I'm forced to file an environmental-impact statement. Only in America do we do this. In China, they don't have environmental-impact statements. They don't even know what that means. And let's say, when I'm planning my project, whether it's a tower, a golf course, a hotel, or whatever it is, there's some kind of toad that we can't kill because it lives there, and we have to protect the toad. What about our jobs? Don't we need to protect those? What about our economy? We need to prioritize jobs and our economy over frogs. Some people will say that is politically incorrect, but I don't care. I don't care about frogs.

So, in America, the environment stands in the way of progress, and you can't build. The project is over. Economic development is over. We can't have it. Therefore, the only way we're ever going to be able to compete and win against countries like China is to completely scrap the environment.

Think of all the services that can easily replace our environment. And they would be even better. They would create a lot of

The environment costs US business an estimated $12 billion per year.

jobs. The hotel industry, for example. Who wouldn't rather stay in a nice hotel than out in the woods? Most of us, I'd say. Why are we preserving the woods and preventing more hotels from being built? It doesn't make any sense. Hotels offer everything the environment can, and a lot more.

Trees are great. I've seen some very nice trees. But do we really need so many? Why do we need to make so much space for them? There's one in my office in a big pot. I like it. But that's plenty of tree. And it should be plenty for anybody. Nobody needs more than one tree. It's time we started thinking about a smarter way to use the land we have on this planet—a great

The environment is clobbering us economically. Doing away with it is something that we have no choice but to consider.

resource. But we can't use it because so much of it is covered with these damned trees.

Do we really need water? There are swimming pools at most of the good hotels. Very nice swimming pools in some of them, and hot tubs—some even

have saunas. These are much nicer places to go than a lake or an ocean. So we don't need those anymore. Do you take a bath indoors, in a bathtub, or do you go into a lake? I think we all know the answer. Get rid of the lake.

Where are you getting your drinking water? If you're getting it from the tap, you don't know what you're doing. Trump-brand Ice spring water is the best drinking water. If we let the city water supplies dry up and instead drink, cook, and shower with Trump Ice, we'll all be a lot better off.

What good is air doing us? We have air conditioning, which is better, and more comfortable than outside air. The quality of

the air-filtration systems in my buildings is the best. It's clean, it's pure. It would not be so expensive to get rid of the Earth's breathable atmosphere and replace it with truly luxury air by providing top-of-the-line air-conditioning and vents that go everywhere. It will be the best air. Don't we deserve the best?

Golf courses will be much nicer with domes over them. They'll be more exclusive—some of the best ones. And you'll never have to worry about weather problems, which will be very nice.

All the time and money we spend "protecting" the environment needs to be focused on building more hotels and office towers, with great restaurants. We'll have all the food and the water and the nice air we need, provided at a very reasonable price. By getting rid of the environment and focusing instead on real economic development, we will not only save trillions that we're now throwing away, we'll build a thriving environment-free economy that's based on innovation, bringing us quality indoor services at a fraction of what the environment is costing us. The environment is such a waste.

We'll go into space one day, and many of the top scientists tell me—this is not me saying this, but them—that there are a lot of other planets like Earth. If we ever need an environment again, which I doubt, then we can go there and get as much of it as we want.

The future for the environment is bright, especially if we can eliminate it by 2050. I challenge the USA and the world to make this vision a reality.

Donald J. Trump is a Republican candidate for president. He is also a New York real-estate developer and former host of NBCs *The Apprentice* **and** *Celebrity Apprentice*. **His most recent book is** *Birds? Fuck 'Em.*

HOW THE EPA SPENDS ITS BUDGET UNDER TRUMP

18%
Exhaust pipe to China

20%
Trump Ice spring water viral-marketing campaign

20%
Money-tree research

2%
Bitchin' Christmas party

15%
Reality show in which companies compete to pump the most carbon dioxide into the atmosphere

12%
Repeatedly dousing small animals with industrial solvent to see what happens

7%
T-shirts for the EPA staff that say, "EPA: Extreme Penis Agility"

5%
Owl removal

Top Trump Tweets

In case climate change is real—and I'm not saying it is—I bought a LOT of Alaskan beach-front property.

• • •

5 WAYS TRUMP CAN MELT THE GLACIERS FASTER

Scientists say our glaciers are melting. Should we believe them? It doesn't matter. The reality is that Donald Trump can melt them faster. Here's how:

1 Aqua Net Super Hold in every Inuit bathroom

2 Glacier-sized tanning beds

3 Set polar bears on fire

4 Drop magma from helicopter

5 Fight and kill Superman, eat Superman's heart, absorb Superman's heat-vision powers, use heat-vision on glaciers

Donald Trump loves nature. That's why he bought a national wildlife preserve and turned it into this beautiful PGA-championship golf course.

Limit immigrant homes to one hour of electricity use per day

Outlaw refrigeration

Strictly regulate energy used by schools, hospitals, and nursing homes

Eliminate wind farms and other energy drains

Only Nevada gets electricity from now on

Instead of electric street lights, set worthless trees on fire

Restrict tanning-bed use to 45 minutes daily (after base tan achieved)

TRUMP'S PLAN TO SAVE ENERGY WITHOUT TURNING OFF A SINGLE NEON CASINO SIGN

Bring back the dinosaurs, kill the dinosaurs, and then harvest their bodies for oil

TRUMP FACT
Trump's carbon footprint is an impressive 12 and a half.

Use new-energy technology to make fuel out of the blood of ISIS children

Build a new sun for half the price of the old sun

Turn off all non-neon-sign electricity at Native American casinos

TRUMP-BRAND WATER: THE NEW OIL

Besides money, water is man's most precious resource. Nobody understands this better than Donald Trump. Under President Trump, America has a sensational policy in place for the preservation and treatment of Trump Ice spring water.

THE HIGHLIGHTS OF TRUMP'S WATER-TREATMENT PLAN

🔖 No matter what, mini-fridge in Oval Office needs to be stocked

🔖 Priority usage in Trump fountains

🔖 Water-treatment plants built to purify water for premium golf-course grass

🔖 Underground water reserves to wash and condition Trump's luxurious hair

🔖 Open Trump-brand ocean desalination plants to stockpile water until market rates are favorable

🔖 Surgical strikes on water-greedy almonds and avocados

🔖 All firefighters will use Trump Ice spring water

This Trump Ice spring water facility near Erie, PA, generates enough water to make Donald Trump a lot of money.

WHAT'S IN DELICIOUS TRUMP ICE SPRING WATER?

- Cost-effective powdered water
- Orange #9
- Testosterone
- Confidence
- Liquefied hair of Ivanka
- Other great, great stuff

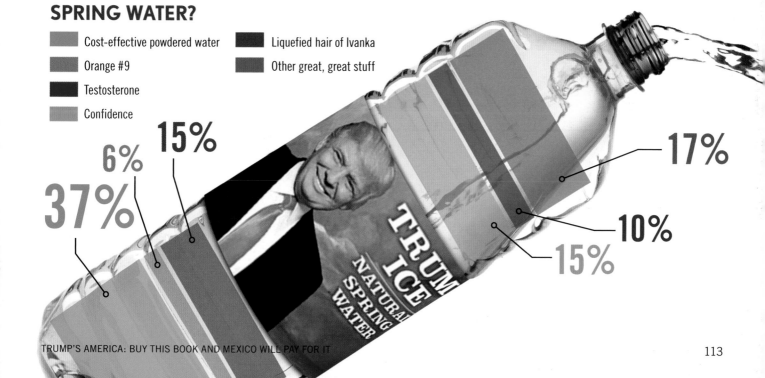

37% 6% 15% 17% 10% 15%

THE GRAND CANYON: IS IT GRAND ENOUGH?

At 277 miles long, 18 miles wide, and over 6,000 feet deep, the Grand Canyon is considered by Donald Trump to be Earth's most magnificent dump. That's why he is proud to select the Trump Organization as the developer for the restoration and transformation of America's most iconic natural attraction.

A BETTER LOCATION

The Grand Canyon is a nice place to visit, but why does it have to be so far away? The project's first priority will be relocating the Grand Canyon to New York City. Situated just north of the Bronx, the Grand Canyon will be a 45-minute shuttle ride from LaGuardia Airport. An increase in visitors will be just the beginning. The canyon will enjoy some long-needed economic development when it's connected by commuter rail to several major northeastern cities.

THE TRUMP RIVER

The Colorado River has not done a particularly good job carving the Grand Canyon. In fact, it's the worst botch job Trump, an experienced builder, has ever seen. Needless to say, it won't be going to New York with the canyon.

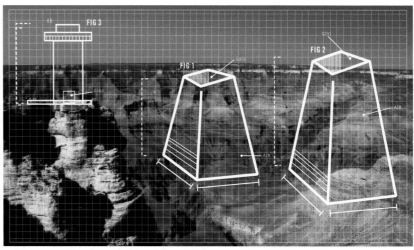

The Trump Grand Canyon features proposed 210-story Trump International Canyon Resort Tower with an observation deck overlooking two new active, man-made volcanoes.

Instead, Trump will introduce the new state-of-the-art Trump River. Sourced exclusively by Trump Ice spring water, the Trump River will not only be the purest, best-tasting river on the planet, but also the fiercest, with underwater jets creating rapids so strong that no one is going to mess with them.

TRUMP INTERNATIONAL CANYON RESORT, GRAND CANYON

Soon to be The Trump Hotel Collection's flagship property, the Trump International Canyon Resort promises to be a spectacular five-star resort, highlighted by the new

Trump International Hotel & Tower. Soaring 210 stories, this diamond-encrusted tower will hold the title of tallest residential building in the world. The tower's panoramic balconies and rooftop deck will offer guests unrivaled views of the Trump Grand Canyon, Trump River, and the Trump National Grand Canyon Golf Links—the world's finest 200-mile, 415-hole championship golf course designed by Jack Nicklaus.

A GRAND FACE-LIFT

Trump has called the Grand Canyon an "eyesore." To give it a makeover befitting the new elegant brand of

America under President Donald Trump, the Grand Canyon will be reshaped into the likeness of Trump's face.

MORE TRUMP

The south, east, and west rims of the canyon will be meticulously chiseled to form Donald's soft chin and jawline. Miles of rolling rock formations will be sculpted to resemble the president's nose and jowl. The Trump River will be routed to accentuate his strong cheekbones. A pair of active, 800-foot titanium volcanoes will serve as Trump's fiery eyes, and his furrowing eyebrows will be suggested with a pair of 11,000-acre weeping-willow forests. For Trump's hair, 750,000 acres of the world's most pristine, golden sand will be flown in from Hawaii and laid along the northern rim of the canyon, emptying all the sand from the Hawaiian island of Kauai.

The Grand Canyon took over 17 million years to form, but the Trump Organization will have the project finished in just 17 days—under budget, too. And while President Trump never understood what was so grand about the Grand Canyon in the first place, he's eager to give it a touch of sophistication and class and transform it into a true natural wonder that's undeniably Trump.

★ ★ ★

1. **Trump River (runs from spring under Trump Mountain)**
2. **Donald Trump Celebratory Presidential Fountain**
3. **Trump Natural Spas**
4. **Trump Grand Canyon Observatory**
5. **Trump Grand Canyon Championship Golf Course**
6. **Future Site of Trump Living National Memorial and Necropolis**
7. **Ivanka Trump Beautiful Nature Trails**
8. **Shops and Food Court**
9. **Parking and Valet Service**
10. **Trump Canyon Adventure Rapids**
11. **Trump Mega-Pool and Lazy River**
12. **Trump Museum, Trump Spooky Castle, and Santrump's Village Tours**

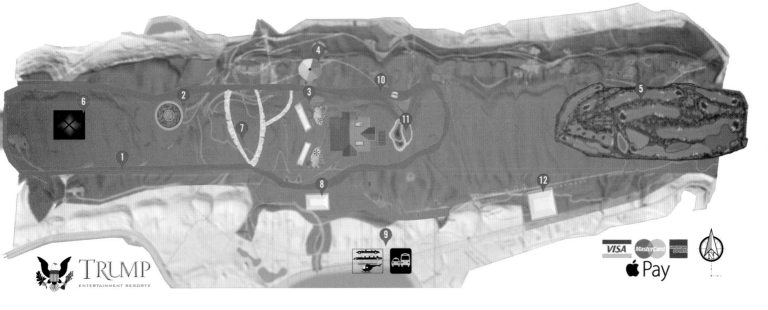

9 Pathetic Species Who Deserve To Go Extinct

Many species on Earth face extinction. These life-forms consume our resources but fail to contribute to the success of any of Donald Trump's businesses. Nor are they doing anything to make America great again. Therefore, our endangered-species laws can't be allowed to protect them. Nature has already made up its mind: they should die.

GIRAFFE
"This is a long-necked horse. Who cares?"

PYRENEAN IBEX
"The name is too complicated to say or write down."

REDWOOD TREE
"It's tall, but I've seen taller. Let's make some cabinets."

FINLESS PORPOISE
"Come back when you have a fin."

STARFISH
"Can't make up its mind whether it's a lousy star or a shitty fish. Next."

BROWN GILLIGAN
"They're all over my golf courses. Get rid of 'em!"

PACIFIC FLIPGROUSE
"They're disgusting and they ought to be dead."

BILLY DOPE
"Billy Dope, you're fired."

MOUNTAIN LUNG PIKA
"This is an animal that has no idea what it's doing. Its time is up."

Top Trump Tweets

I'll take all the money we're wasting on climate change and use it to clone dinosaurs.

. . .

THE ENVIRONMENT: HIPPIE CRAP

TRUMP'S GUIDE TO PROFITABLY SOURCED SEAFOOD

Every day, global populations of fish are caught and sold at alarmingly low profit margins. To ensure you're eating only the most sustainably lucrative seafood and doing your part to preserve the financial health of our nation's commercial-fishing interests—one of whom is Donald Trump—use this helpful guide when making your menu selection.

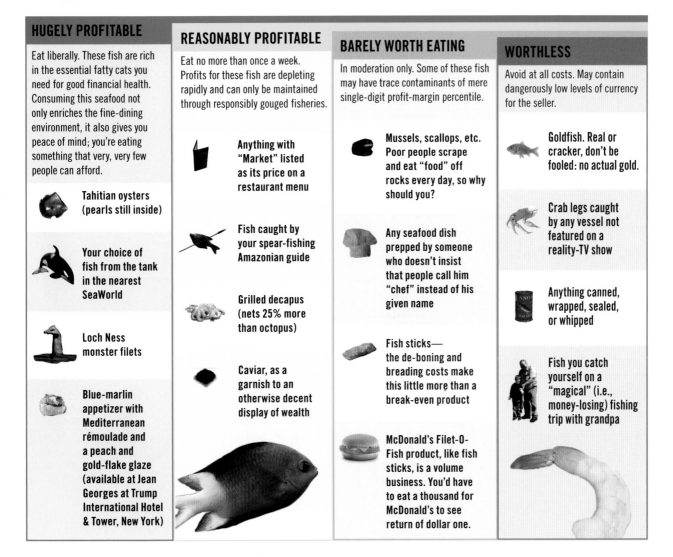

HUGELY PROFITABLE

Eat liberally. These fish are rich in the essential fatty cats you need for good financial health. Consuming this seafood not only enriches the fine-dining environment, it also gives you peace of mind; you're eating something that very, very few people can afford.

- Tahitian oysters (pearls still inside)

- Your choice of fish from the tank in the nearest SeaWorld

- Loch Ness monster filets

- Blue-marlin appetizer with Mediterranean rémoulade and a peach and gold-flake glaze (available at Jean Georges at Trump International Hotel & Tower, New York)

REASONABLY PROFITABLE

Eat no more than once a week. Profits for these fish are depleting rapidly and can only be maintained through responsibly gouged fisheries.

- Anything with "Market" listed as its price on a restaurant menu

- Fish caught by your spear-fishing Amazonian guide

- Grilled decapus (nets 25% more than octopus)

- Caviar, as a garnish to an otherwise decent display of wealth

BARELY WORTH EATING

In moderation only. Some of these fish may have trace contaminants of mere single-digit profit-margin percentile.

- Mussels, scallops, etc. Poor people scrape and eat "food" off rocks every day, so why should you?

- Any seafood dish prepped by someone who doesn't insist that people call him "chef" instead of his given name

- Fish sticks— the de-boning and breading costs make this little more than a break-even product

- McDonald's Filet-O-Fish product, like fish sticks, is a volume business. You'd have to eat a thousand for McDonald's to see return of dollar one.

WORTHLESS

Avoid at all costs. May contain dangerously low levels of currency for the seller.

- Goldfish. Real or cracker, don't be fooled: no actual gold.

- Crab legs caught by any vessel not featured on a reality-TV show

- Anything canned, wrapped, sealed, or whipped

- Fish you catch yourself on a "magical" (i.e., money-losing) fishing trip with grandpa

DONALD TRUMP, EARTH-FRIENDLY HERO

To capitalize on kids' naive interest in saving the environment, Trump partnered with Japanese comics conglomerate Shogakukan to create *Trump's Green Winners*, a four-part action series that shows how we can bring the environment to heel in the interest of commerce. It features a super-strong, super-genius Trump and his family saving the planet Earth's profit potential and showing tough love to doomed species he knows he can turn into winners. Comic-book Trump—and real-life Trump—made millions in the process.

Trump's Green Winners #3, August 2009

HOW TO COME OUT ON TOP, SAVE FACE, AND LOOK INCREDIBLE AFTER THE NUCLEAR WARS

The nuclear wars are probably going to happen. There are simply too many crazy world leaders with their finger on the button to expect anything less. The only real question is, which madman will press it first? President Trump may decide to prevent that horrible fate by striking preemptively, just to be prudent. No matter how the nuclear fire rains down on the world, you can rest assured Trump will do everything he can to make sure he—and possibly you, too—comes out a winner.

 BUILD A LUXURIOUS FALLOUT SHELTER LIKE TRUMP'S Lined with 7 feet of solid gold and equipped with a sensual radiation bath/Jacuzzi, tanning bed, and Success By Trump® cologne-filtration system, Donald Trump's fallout shelter will ensure he and his family are not only safe, but pampered—for decades, if necessary.

 HELP OTHERS BY ASSURING THEM TRUMP IS OKAY Trump will broadcast live readings of his Twitter feed to any mutants or roving cannibal militias who are able to receive his signal. These desperate throngs will be sick with worry about the state of Donald Trump. As you evade violent gangs and deadly contamination, be sure to prioritize a search for existing Wi-Fi hotspots so you can assure your loved ones Donald Trump and his family are extremely comfortable.

 REBUILD AMERICA, BIGGER AND BETTER THAN BEFORE Instead of fleeing uninhabitable wastelands, take charge of rebuilding a radiated America and making it even greater. That's what Donald Trump will do. He'll summon his prowess as a successful real-estate developer to build enormous skyscrapers that will tower over the radiation clouds and diseased hordes. He will make many billions of dollars renting luxury apartments, rousing Americans—and the entire world—to cheer his great success once again.

 REPOPULATE THE COUNTRY Help collect the world's remaining beautiful, unmutated women and present them to Trump, who will offer his precious seed to as many of these lucky women as possible. (Some mutants may be allowed if their mutation makes them sexier, like the blue lady from *X-Men*.) Additionally, Trump-brand semen will be marketed as a premium product for discerning survivors who want to produce uninfected winners. In fact, Trump has already begun collecting ejaculate in anticipation of the frenzied demand. Reserve your order online now at www.trumpseed.com.

THE BEST TRUMP-BRAND SOAPS FOR WASHING OFF RADIATION

Nagasaki Spring

Silkwood Scrub

Neutroshima

Kiss My Raw Bleeding Face

Dr. Oppenheimer's

Bombs of Maine

SCIENCE

"IF EINSTEIN WAS SO SMART, WHY WASN'T HE RICH?"

SOME SCIENCE IS GREAT, SOME SCIENCE IS GARBAGE

Donald Trump has always appreciated science that gets results, and that won't change now that he's president. This draft speech to the National Science Foundation offers a unique glimpse into how important science is in a Trump administration.

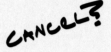

THE WHITE HOUSE
WASHINGTON

SPEECH TO NATIONAL SCIENCE FOUNDATION *CANCEL?*

I like science. Science has been great for me. Gravity, I love. If it wasn't for gravity, golf would be impossible.

But there are a lot of scientists—not all of them, but some—who are trying to sell us a bill of goods.

We're not buying it anymore.

Some science is true, and some is not. Some science is fiction. And I'm not talking about the good kind with the good-looking alien women. I'm talking about so-called science that's nothing but a lot of nonsense.

We've made some very stupid investments in science. I don't like bad investments, clearly. (I'm worth billions.) Now, I'm not saying we should completely abolish all science. At least, not now. But something's got to be done. We need a new approach.

So, it's time to put science, and the scientists who do it, on notice in our country. We need someone to look over their findings. What science needs is a strong leader.

The point is, Americans are being told a lot of garbage that isn't science. As President, I'm going to do somehing about it. What's going to happen is we're going to get tough on science. We're going to show it who's in charge. And in the end, a few eggheads might get fired. Big deal.

[AD LIB]

Top Trump Tweets

Trump, not science, Is worth 10 billion dollars.

. . .

TRUMP TIP
If you are ever confronted with a science, do not run. Spread your arms to make yourself look bigger and shout at the science until it retreats.

SCIENCE: "IF EINSTEIN WAS SO SMART, WHY WASN'T HE RICH?"

TRUMP'S UPGRADED PERIODIC TABLE OF ELEMENTS

1 H HYDROGEN 1.00794																	2 He HELIUM 4.0026
3 Li LITHIUM 6.941	4 Be BERYLLIUM 9.0122											5 B BORON 10.811	6 C CARBON 12.011	7 N NITROGEN 14.007	8 O OXYGEN 15.999	9 F FLUORINE 18.998	10 Ne NEON 20.17
11 Na SODIUM 22.990	12 Mg MAGNESIUM 24.305											13 Al ALUMINIUM 26.982	14 Si SILICON 28.0	15 P PHOSPHOR 30.4	16 S SULPHUR 32.065	17 Cl CHLORINE 35.453	18 Ar ARGON 39.948
19 K POTASSIUM 39.098	20 Ca CALCIUM 40.078	21 Sc SCANDIUM 44.956	22 Ti TITANIUM 47.867	23 V VANADIUM 50.942	24 Cr CHROMIUM 51.996	25 Mn MANGANESE 54.938	26 Fe IRON 55.845	27 Co COBALT 58.933	28 Ni NICKEL 58.693	29 Cu COPPER 63.546	30 Zn ZINC 65.38	31 Ga GALLIUM 69.723	32 Ge GERMANIUM 72.64	33 As ARSENIC 74.922	34 Se SELENIUM 78.96	35 Br BROMINE 79.904	36 Kr KRYPTON 83.798
37 Rb RUBIDIUM 85.4670	38 Sr STRONTIUM 87.62	39 Y YTTRIUM 88.906	40 Zr ZIRCONIUM 91.224	41 Nb NIOBIUM 92.906	42 Mo MOLYBDENUM 95.94	43 Tc TECHNETIUM (98)	44 Ru NAME MASS	45 Rh NAME MASS	46 Pd PALLADIUM 106.42	47 Ag SILVER	48 Cd CADMIUM 112.41	49 In INDIUM 114.82	50 Sn TIN 116.71	51 Sb ANTIMONY 121.60	52 Te TELLURIUM 127.76	53 I IODINE 126.90	54 Xe XENON 131.293
55 Cs CAESIUM 132.91	56 Ba BARIUM 137.33	57–71 LANTHANIDE	72 Hf HAFNIUM 178.49	73 Ta TANTALUM 18.95	74 W TUNGSTEN 183.84	75 Re RHENIUM 186.21	76 Os OSMIUM 190.23	77 Ir IRIDIUM 192.22	78 Pt PLATINUM 195.08	79 Au GOLD	80 Hg MERCURY 200.59	81 Tl THALLIUM 204.38	82 Pb LEAD 207.0	83 Bi BISMUTH 208.98	84 Po POLONIUM (209)	85 At ASTATINE (210)	86 Rn RADON 222.0176
87 Fr FRANCIUM (223)	88 Ra RADIUM (226)	89–103 ACTINIDE	104 Rf RUTHERFORDIUM (261)	105 Db DUBNIUM (262)	106 Sg SEABORGIUM (266)	107 Bh BOHRIUM (264)	108 Hs HASSIUM (277)	109 Mt MEITNERIUM (268)	110 Uun UNUNNILIUM (281)	111 Uuu UNUNUNIUM (281)	112 Uub UNUNBIUM (285)	113 Uut UNUNTRIUM	114 Uuq UNUNQUADIUM (289)	115 Uup UNUNPENTIUM (288)	116 Uuh UNUNHEXIUM (292)	117 Uus UNUNSEPTIUM (?)	118 Uuo UNUNOCTIUM (294)

57 La LANTHANUM 138.91	58 Ce CERIUM 140.12	59 Pr PRASEODYMIUM 140.91	60 Nd NEODYMIUM 144.24	61 Pm PROMETHIUM (145)	62 Sm SAMARIUM 150.36	63 Eu EUROPIUM 151.96	64 Gd GADOLINIUM 157.25	65 Tb TERBIUM 158.93	66 Dy DYSPROSIUM 162.50	67 Ho HOLMIUM 164.93	68 Er ERBIUM 167.26	69 Tm THULIUM 168.93	70 Yb YTTERBIUM 173.04	71 Lu LUTATIUM 174.9558
89 Ac ACTINIUM (227)	90 Th THORIUM 232.04	91 Pa PROTACTINIUM 231.04	92 U URANIUM 238.03	93 Np NEPTUNIUM	94 Pu PLUTONIUM (244)	95 Am AMERICIUM (243)	96 Cm CURIUM (247)	97 Bk BERKELIUM (247)	98 Cf CALIFORNIUM (251)	99 Es EINSTEINIUM (252)	100 Fm FERMIUM (257)	101 Md MENDELEVIUM (258)	102 No NOBELIUM (259)	103 Lr LAWRENCIUM (262)

TRUMP'S ADDITIONS

Tr TRUMPTANIUM	Ad ARTOFDEALIUM						Me MELANIUM	Hc HELICOPTORON	Vi VIRILIUM
Ma MANHATTONITE	Eg EGOMANIUM	Tu TRUSTFUNDON	Op OPPORTUNION	Bi BILLION	Lm LIMOUSINIUM	Cn CONDOMINIUM	Iv IVANKIUM	Di DIVORCIUM	Ph PHALLIUM
$$ CLASSIUM	Xn XENOPHOBIUM	Tg TRUMPGREAT	Wh CREST-WHITESTRIP	Ml MAR-A-LARGON	Yu YUUUGIUM	#T HASHTAGIUM	Sg SUPERGOLD	Pr PRENUPTON	Lo LOSERON

A SMARTER SCIENTIFIC METHOD

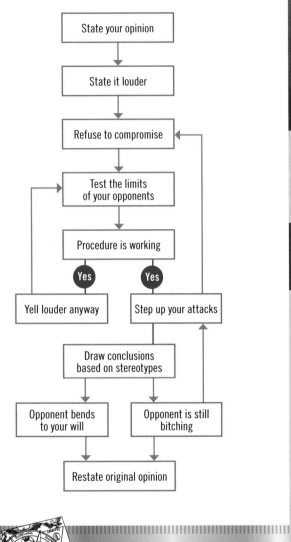

```
┌─────────────────────┐
│  State your opinion  │
└─────────────────────┘
           ↓
┌─────────────────────┐
│   State it louder    │
└─────────────────────┘
           ↓
┌─────────────────────┐
│ Refuse to compromise │◄──────┐
└─────────────────────┘       │
           ↓                   │
┌─────────────────────┐       │
│   Test the limits    │       │
│  of your opponents   │       │
└─────────────────────┘       │
           ↓                   │
┌─────────────────────┐       │
│ Procedure is working │       │
└─────────────────────┘       │
     (Yes)      (Yes)          │
       ↓          ↓            │
┌───────────┐ ┌──────────────┐│
│Yell louder│ │Step up your  ││
│  anyway   │ │   attacks    ││
└───────────┘ └──────────────┘│
       │          ↑            │
       ↓      ┌──────────────┐ │
┌─────────────│Draw conclusions│
│   based on stereotypes     │
└─────────────────────────────┘
       ↓          ↓
┌───────────┐ ┌──────────────┐
│Opponent   │ │Opponent is   │
│bends to   │ │still bitching│
│your will  │ │              │
└───────────┘ └──────────────┘
       ↓          ↓
┌─────────────────────────────┐
│  Restate original opinion   │
└─────────────────────────────┘
```

TRUMP FACT
President Trump invests heavily in the American alchemy industry.

THE SCIENTIFIC METHOD: AN INEFFECTIVE BUSINESS MODEL

> **"We need to teach our scientists to make deals." – Donald Trump**

Science has given us modern medicine and lightweight carbon-fiber golf clubs. Its strength lies in great minds like Galileo and Newton who reveal new truths and unleash periodic scientific advancements. But now it's time to hand the reins of science to someone who can actually get things done—Donald Trump.

No longer will researchers fritter away taxpayer dollars on an endless cycle of observation, hypothesizing, experimentation, and critical analysis. According to Trump, "They'll stop wasting time on repetitive experiments and spend more time thinking about return on investment."

"We need to teach our scientists to make deals," Trump says. "Big deals." As president, Trump directs scientists from both government and public universities to consider ways their science can generate revenue, or else. Says Trump, "If NASA's going to build a spaceship, they'd better make regular trips to someplace exciting, and they'd better sell a lot of tickets."

Trump predicts that scientific money holes like astronomy, ecology, and anthropology will be operating at a healthy surplus by 2018.

SCIENCE: "IF EINSTEIN WAS SO SMART, WHY WASN'T HE RICH?"

BRANCHES OF SCIENCE RANKED BY EARNING POWER

1. ASTRONOMY. Earning power: $104,245 per year

"An astronomer is someone who failed at becoming an astronaut. They're paid mostly out of pity."

2. PHYSICS. Earning power: $88,525 per year

"Physicists have the power to create a black hole and destroy the universe, so they get paid a decent amount to keep them from doing that."

3. GEOLOGY. Earning power: $68,052 per year

"The study of what's in the ground is important because that's where oil is, but they don't get paid a lot. You're a lot better off becoming an oil baron."

4. BIOLOGY. Earning power: $67,940 per year

"Biology is all about instinct. No need for this field."

5. MICROBIOLOGY. Earning power: $63,908 per year

"Just a smaller, harder-to-see version of biology. Pathetic."

The New York Times, February 17, 2017

TRUMP CALLS ON TOP ELEVATOR ENGINEERS

URGENT ACTION NEEDED

'We Must Make My Ride Up Trump Tower Smoother'

By STEPHEN KIRSCHENBAUM

NEW YORK—Calling it the most critical challenge facing modern science, President Trump announced today he had begun a search for the world's foremost engineers to help make his elevator ride in Trump Tower a little smoother. "On behalf of the American people, I ask the world's top engineers to rise up and achieve this pinnacle of engineering achievement," Trump told a crowd of reporters gathered in Trump Tower's elevator bank. "I take this elevator all the time, and don't get me wrong, it is a very smooth ride, believe me—one of the best. [The] cables alone cost millions," he said. "But we can not rest until it is the very best."

The president provided some specifics for his vision, including a call to "create, before this decade is out, a Trump Tower elevator ascent that is more cloud-like." President Trump acknowledged one challenge in the mission: the little bump he feels around floor 55.

"This will not be easy, but being the best never is," he said.

The president said the project would inspire future generations of Americans, who he predicts will beam with pride when they hear stories of the current generation's most brilliant minds coming together to lift him hundreds of feet into the air without a noticeable teeter or jostle.

Washington Post, September 4, 2022

President congratulates astronauts on 'meaningless journey'

BY LEWIS HAMMOND

WASHINGTON—In a phone call from the Oval Office today, President Trump welcomed three astronauts who returned from a trip to deep space Friday, docking at the International Space Station. He congratulated them for their "pointless and dumb" trip.

"Earth is the greatest planet in history—nothing else comes close," the president said during the one-minute call with explorers Steven Adlard, Lee Traynor, and Kenneth Drewell. "You risked your lives to leave Earth to go into the empty nothingness of space. And for what?"

The president chided the astronauts for visiting outer space when there are better places to explore on Earth. "But seriously," he said, "who among us hasn't stared up at the night sky, realized what a waste of time that is, and then gotten back to work?"

Trump ended the call by explaining that the astronauts were no longer needed and would be fired immediately upon their return to Earth tomorrow afternoon.

ASTRONAUTS CONTINUED ON A6

NASA

President Trump speaks with the astronauts over NASA videolink.

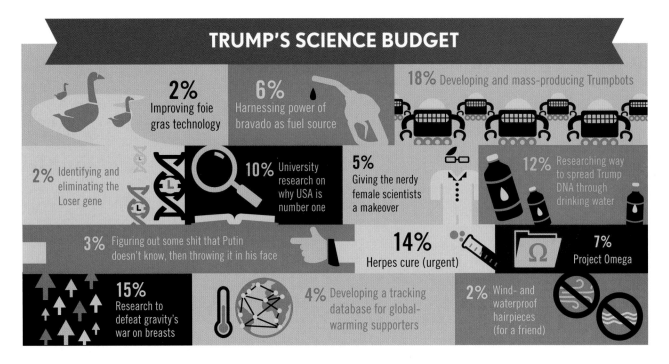

TRUMP'S SCIENCE BUDGET

2% Improving foie gras technology

6% Harnessing power of bravado as fuel source

18% Developing and mass-producing Trumpbots

2% Identifying and eliminating the Loser gene

10% University research on why USA is number one

5% Giving the nerdy female scientists a makeover

12% Researching way to spread Trump DNA through drinking water

3% Figuring out some shit that Putin doesn't know, then throwing it in his face

14% Herpes cure (urgent)

7% Project Omega

15% Research to defeat gravity's war on breasts

4% Developing a tracking database for global-warming supporters

2% Wind- and waterproof hairpieces (for a friend)

Washington Post, April 16, 2023

Trump awards chemist who explained why women find Trump irresistible

BY MIRIAM BILLINGS

A leading researcher in Trump sexual chemistry received the National Medal of Science from President Trump at a Rose Garden Ceremony Saturday. The recipient, Dr. Gerald Templeton, has published several papers quantifying President Trump's immensely powerful sex appeal with women, work that may help future researchers comprehend and ultimately understand the raw sexual allure of Trump.

Trump praised the Scripps Research Institute chemist for "shedding light on one of the great mysteries of our time." He urged more chemists to join the research, and called on young people to pursue careers in science so that the matter can be investigated and written about for decades to come.

Templeton remarked that the medal, the highest tribute the president can award for distinguished scientific achievement, will help scientists understand the power of Trump's appeal to women, especially those who are 8s or higher.

In his research, funded by a special White House science grant, Templeton conducted interviews with Trump's wife and ex-wives, logging volumes of data on Trump's sexual magnetism and dangerous sexual electricity. He also conducted several studies in which Trump, who cleared his schedule last fall to participate, was placed in close contact with hundreds of women. In in-depth interviews, Templeton found that the small percentage who were able to resist Trump's charm were independently described by Trump as either "manly" or "confused."

At the ceremony, Trump announced a new scientific grant program to investigate why he is so virile for his age.

Top Trump Tweets

The solution to so-called Global Warming is as simple as getting scientists to shut up.

. . .

A Mars Rover begins construction on Trump Tower Mars.

MARS IS BEATING US. HOW CAN WE WIN?

American scientists have sent Mars expensive robots, rockets, and fancy cameras. But what have we gotten in return? Nothing. Trump has made it clear the "chuckleheads" at NASA don't know what they're doing. Says Trump: "Mars is laughing at us and pushing us around, and it's time to change the rules of the game."

Trump has proposed several ways to start getting payback from Mars today.

★ Build ultra Mars space laser pointed at Earth to aid in international negotiations

★ Bring back Martian rocks to throw at illegals trying to climb the wall

★ Send second rover to Mars to fight the first rover, sell the footage

★ Send Muslims to colonize Mars and mine potential resources

★ Fill canyons with Trump Ice spring water to create life

Regardless of the outcome, Mars is on notice. Trump has pledged that if our Red Planet fortunes can't be turned around, he will blow it up.

THE PLANETS RANKED BY TRUMP

1. JUPITER
"The biggest, the best."

2. SATURN
"I respect it."

3. EARTH
"The smartest. Who's got robots all over space? Not Mercury."

4. PLUTO
"Unfairly disgraced by the politically correct science police. Still a planet."

5. NEPTUNE
"I don't have time for Neptune."

6. MARS
"A disappointment."

7. URANUS
"Grow up."

8. VENUS
"Not buying it."

9. MERCURY
"A joke."

WOMEN: WHAT ARE THEY?

The bedroom. The workplace. Frozen-yogurt shops. Women can be found just about anywhere. But what are they, and how can we cherish them? In Trump's America, this is an important pursuit.

THE DIFFERENT TYPES

Women come in all different shapes and sizes, some attractive, some not. All can be volatile, emotionally explosive, and critical. Trump has had many run-ins with angry women, and he's handled each one with grace and self-control thanks to his sensitivity and sex appeal—essential qualities when dealing with women and the controversial issues that surround them.

YOGA AND HOW TO AVOID IT

You may have heard of yoga and even been intrigued by the sight of women stretching in tight pants, but beware. Yoga encourages women to promote meditation, a vegetarian lifestyle, and even gluten-free food. Women can be very persuasive, and if you express any interest in yoga, it's likely that you will never be served steak again. Firmly reject any invitations to participate.

WINNING ARGUMENTS WITH WOMEN

Irate women who suffer from what Sigmund Freud called "penis envy" often try to draw Trump into arguments. Trump is able to defeat these efforts with deal-making skills. But how can you?

First, compliment the woman by comparing her to a pig or a dog. These are animals that are traditionally revered for their intelligence, usefulness, and adorable antics. Women take this as a great compliment. Next, suggest that the woman might be experiencing mood shifts due to her menstrual cycle. This is a helpful reminder that women suffer from a shameful biological side effect of being a woman, and it shows that you sympathize with them. Finally, rate her looks on a scale of 1–10. Women love to be told how beautiful they are, and they appreciate honesty. This will also let a woman know where she ranks on your personal attractiveness meter, and whether she has a chance at being taken to dinner by you. If you think an argument is over, don't stop. Continue arguments for years. Women like to know that you're still thinking about them, even after they've moved on with their lives.

A COST ANALYSIS

What's the bottom line when it comes to women? Money is often something women can be seen whining about, but the truth is, they can be costly, and many are not worth the investment. Mathematically speaking, the number of back rubs, foot rubs, and intercourse you receive from a woman is proportional to the amount of money you spend. Marriage is a different set of financial risks, but a prenuptial agreement can reduce your losses.

TRUMP FACT
Trump can bench whatever you can bench, plus 10 pounds.

SCIENCE: "IF EINSTEIN WAS SO SMART, WHY WASN'T HE RICH?"

How To Make Superior Children Using The Patented Trump Elite Conception Method

Not only is procreation an essential component of capitalism, it's downright fun. But all those mind-blowing orgasms are for nothing if you don't produce fine, strong, American children. The United States is behind China in the production of children. So, in order to make America great again, Donald Trump has created a mating process guaranteed to produce superior offspring without failure every time.

STEP 1 Get her in the mood. A candlelit dinner in the Trump Plaza Hotel honeymoon suite should do the trick.

STEP 2 Foreplay. Not that important. Time is money.

STEP 3 Position the woman on a Trumpurepedic bed made with satin sheets with a thread count of no less than 1,200. After she has signed your Declaration of Optimal Menstrual Cycle Timing agreement, she must be placed on her back, ankles behind the neck in a gentle, loving contortion. This ensures the semen will be deposited and drained directly into the uterus without any chance of leakage.

STEP 4 Position yourself in a horizontal teeter-totter stance using the supermodel's hips as a fulcrum.

STEP 5 Rotate in a clockwise motion. Gain momentum as you spin. Your intertwined bodies should resemble Trump's private helicopter taking off to an important business conference downtown.

STEP 6 Ejaculate at precisely 7 to 9 minutes after Step 4 re-entry. A child conceived at this juncture will be born with the drive necessary to succeed in the resort, gaming, or reality-TV fields.

STEP 7 Cuddle. 20 seconds maximum. Get back to work.

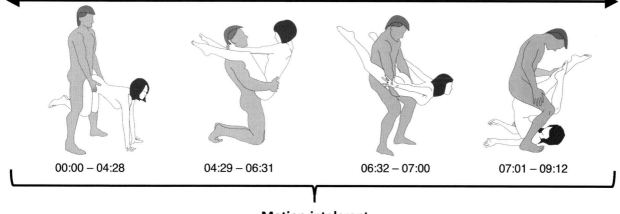

Flexion-intolerant   **Copulation Variance Schedule**   **Extension-intolerant**

00:00 – 04:28   04:29 – 06:31   06:32 – 07:00   07:01 – 09:12

Motion-intolerant

NEW TRUMP-ERA GADGETS

Buckle up! The speed of technology with President Trump in office will be blinding due to the unending stream of victories American companies will enjoy. Here's just a sampling of Trump's "world of tomorrow."

THE MEXIBOT

With our border sealed, who will bus our tables, mow our lawns, and wash our cars? The Mexibot, naturally. Just as hard working as the illegal help you're used to, this obedient mechanical servant is also clean, speaks English, and is guaranteed to never rape you. (A malfunctioning Mexibot may rape you.)

NANO-TRUMPS

Tiny Donald Trumps will win on a subatomic level. Have prostate cancer? Nano-Trumps will blast your tumor. And while they're in you, they'll increase the length of your penis, too. Women will enjoy surprise pregnancies with the best babies.

THE VERY SMART PHONE

It's time for America to realize that the so-called "smart" phones of today are stupid. Our phones should diagnose and cure disease, teleport us anywhere in the galaxy, and have a "stun" and "kill" setting. Rest assured, with Trump as president, they will.

TRUMP-BRAND PROTEIN PASTE

After the Trump Gene Wars have destroyed all the livestock and crops, this miracle food will feed the world. What will it be made of? Well, Trump won't divulge the recipe, but one thing is for sure—it won't be ground-up undesirables, no matter what everyone says. However, vegetarians may want to avoid the food and subsist instead on the underground breast-milk market.

Top Trump Tweets

Fact: More wind farms since the 1970s. Same percentage increase in Leukemia. #NoCoincidence

• • •

WHAT'S IN OUR CHILDREN'S VACCINES?

★ Autism
★ Expensive placebos
★ An admission that your child is too weak to fight off polio himself
★ The foolish worries of women
★ Doctors' lies
★ An FDA-approved level of rat feces

TRUMP FACT
Donald Trump sells a Trump-brand luxury vaccine, and recommends parents test it on their children.

SCIENCE: "IF EINSTEIN WAS SO SMART, WHY WASN'T HE RICH?"

POISON CONTROL

How Trump Gained Immunity To 400 Different Poisons, And How You Can Too

1 Ingest 8 ounces of poison on an empty stomach.

2 Don't ask for help. The poison will sense weakness.

3 Stay awake. Poison doesn't sleep. Neither should you.

4 Initiate rolling blackouts of your internal organs. Shut down the spleen. When the poison shows up, it will see it's closed for business and move on to the liver. Fire up the spleen and shut down the liver. Keep the poison guessing.

5 Invite the poison on a conference call. The poison will get so bored it will die. Nothing gets done on a conference call.

6 Take more poison. Turn your body into a death cage where the poisons turn on each other.

7 Poison the poison. Turn the tables and give the poison a lethal dose of you. Two can play at this game.

POISON	EFFECT ON TRUMP
Bleach	*Mild buzz*
Drano	*The giggles*
Strychnine	*Itching*
Cyanide	*Sudden desire to polish goldware*
Weed killer	*Momentary sensation of empathy*
Lead	*36-hour erection*
Ricin	*X-ray vision*
Hemlock	*Ability to solve crimes*
Agent Orange	*Healthy glow*
Gamma rays	*Turn green, but same personality*
Sarin gas	*Heightened awareness of bad deals*
Anthrax	*Urge to press red buttons*

NASA's New Mission: To Search For Interstellar Candidates For The Miss Universe Pageant

President Donald Trump has issued a bold challenge to NASA: to end the decades-old Earth bias in the selection of the most beautiful woman in the universe. Trump will lead humanity in a new era of both space exploration and the judging of female excellence. He will call on NASA to begin an extensive search through the vast reaches of outer space to find contestants stunning enough to give Earth women some serious competition.

NASA scientists will recalibrate their radio signals, adjust the Kepler and Hubble space telescopes, and finely tune all other instruments to scan the near-ultraviolet, visible, and near-infrared spectra beyond Earth for the most "amazing looking" and "elegant" female aliens.

"We need to look for any sign of life on other planets that's got that classic hourglass shape, and has some element of poise—that's what we're really going to be looking for," Trump says.

NASA scientists have already found several Earth-like planets outside our solar system that many believe contain the elements necessary to sustain gorgeous extraterrestrial life.

KEPLER-186F

Barely within its star's "habitable zone," this planet's beauty contestants are likely composed of frozen nitrogen.

KEPLER 62E

This oceanic planet has plenty of water to hydrate any life-forms, likely resulting in radiant alien skin.

KEPLER 62F

Miss Universe officials say this close neighbor of Kepler 62e may already judge female organisms from both planets, making for competitors already familiar with universe-wide pageant rules.

GLIESE 667CC

With high temperatures due to its close orbit around a red sun, this planet, according to NASA Interstellar Researcher Tim Kitagawa, may literally offer "sizzling hot babes."

The Search For Extraterrestrial Beauties

Need to find the planet Princess Leia is from and confirm it was only blown up in the movie and not in real life

DEEP SPACE

Maybe this is where those chicks from Star Trek are

Scientists advised to avoid crab nebula

Donald Trump's circa-1984 headshot will be beamed into space to lure the most attractive alien ladies

Radio signals to alien beauties will be sent along with a dozen roses

Finalists will have the opportunity to be rocketed to Mercury to tan up before the swimsuit competition

Sensors will be calibrated to detect as high as a "10"

EARTH

Scientists will be advised to skip the misleadingly named Venus—no women

"Hubba-Hubba" Telescope

Search will avoid planets with rings or which seem overeager to acquire rings

Black holes hold tremendous potential in the search for additional contestants. Known to be portals to parallel universes, black holes would likely produce many alternate-universe versions of the most beautiful lifeforms. To take advantage of this resource, our best scientists will need to create new technologies capable of not only transporting beauty contestants, but preemptively eliminating any competition from their counterparts. President Trump, in order to maintain his status as a world leader and advisor to the Miss Universe pageant, will also need special technology to kill any alternate-universe President Trumps.

Tryouts will take place on the moon before contestants are eligible for Earth competition.

Milk, plasma, or whatever the potential contestants secrete will be examined in a lab for its potency of elements and value of matter, and then drunk by Donald Trump. Contestants will be chosen after he judges the taste.

President Trump will appoint William Shatner to lead the search for interstellar babes.

"WE MUST FIND AND DEFEAT BIGFOOT"

Trump has vowed to locate and eradicate the most dangerous individual threat to American safety and security: Bigfoot. A danger particularly to residents of our nation's beautiful wooded areas, Bigfoot, Trump believes, must be eliminated in order to protect all Americans from the creature's unprecedented reign of terror.

 "WE'VE GOT TO FIND HIM, ONCE AND FOR ALL, AND GET RID OF HIM."

Trump offers the following essential steps for ending Bigfoot's decades-long menace to civilized society:

1. Cut off access to his most important assets: fruit and small game. Trump recommends knocking out all the edible berries in the area by sending in large teams of experienced pickers to pick all the bushes clean. Then, take all the rabbits out of the woods with large nets. Once Bigfoot is starved out, Trump believes all those berries and rabbits ought to be given back to Americans.

 "THAT MONKEY-MAN IS OUT THERE LAUGHING AT US."

2. Trump believes Bigfoot's biggest vulnerability is his trust in other animals who may be unlawfully harboring him. A reward must be offered to any

 "IS HE MAN OR BEAST, OR PART MAN, PART BEAST? NOBODY KNOWS. AND THE SO-CALLED EXPERTS HAVE GOTTEN US NOWHERE."

bear, elk, or puma who will divulge Bigfoot's whereabouts to U.S. authorities. Rewards to consider are food, safe passage, or an opportunity to join the circus. Once Bigfoot is alone and friendless in his vast wooded refuge, he will be much easier to capture.

3. Finally, Trump advises a strong military approach. This leaves nothing to chance. If Bigfoot hasn't

already given himself up after the first two steps, he'll certainly be crushed by the U.S. military, aided by local militias if necessary. Troops will sweep the woods, banging on pots and pans and yelling slurs and insults at Bigfoot to not only flush him out, but destroy his will to live. They'll follow with a slash and burn, leaving Bigfoot's formerly tranquil home in ashes.

 "BIGFOOT IS AMERICA'S BIGGEST PROBLEM THAT NOBODY TALKS ABOUT."

Trump promises to implement this solution to the Bigfoot menace within his first 100 days as president. He further guarantees that, as an avid hunter, he will finish the job himself. Once Bigfoot is weak, hungry, subdued, and whimpering at Trump's feet, Trump will look into the mongrel's eyes and personally shoot him in the face.

In a world without Bigfoot, Americans will once again venture into our state and national parks to enjoy all the natural beauty and splendor they offer, without fear that a hideous monster will be lurking in the distance. Because that monster will be dead.

Top Trump Tweets

We need another WWII so we can steal another batch of Nazi rocket scientists.

• • •

Study Suggests Benefits of Playing 'Art of the Deal' Audiobook to Unborn

By PATRICIA GOODWIN and HARRIS TULEGUARDE

The authors of a study published in The New England Journal of Medicine have found evidence suggesting playing the audiobook of Donald Trump's "The Art of the Deal" to babies while in the womb can have significant cognitive, physical, and emotional benefits.

"Many parents have long believed, without supporting evidence, that playing classical music to a fetus might somehow enhance brain development," lead researcher Danielle Blair said. "However, our study showed conclusively that playing 'The Art of the Deal' audiobook was more effective than Mozart, Haydn, or Bach."

Ms. Blair's study, ongoing since 2015, has found that no music of the classical composers or even the voice of an unborn child's parents are as effective as Mr. Trump's voice at growing healthier, more confident, and better-looking children.

Anecdotally, many new parents have reported remarkable qualities in children who listened to "The Art of the Deal" while in the womb. Sherry Wordstrom, a mother in Pasadena, wrote in her parenting blog "Trump Youth" that her newborn son Avery began pounding his fists on top of desks as early as six months, and had learned to negotiate for longer breast-feedings even younger than that.

"My son is smarter, stronger, and more successful than other babies," she said. "In short, he wins."

Among the benefits specified by the study, playing the audiobook to fetuses led to increased self-confidence, an increased ability to make and close deals, and an intrinsic understanding of the high-end New York real-estate market.

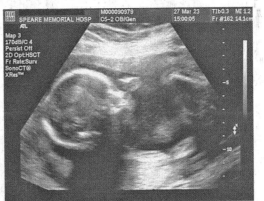

KATHRYN SEYMOUR / THE NEW YORK TIMES

Bred for Success
In a years-long study, fetal brains exposed to the voice of Donald Trump reading the unabridged "The Art of the Deal" audiobook showed marked increases over control groups in cognitive function under pressure, intuition, and high-stakes deal-making.

HOW TO KILL MONSTERS

There are terrifying spectres in this world, things that live in the darkness. You may never encounter one, but if you do, you'd better be prepared. Donald Trump has spent his life fighting these evils. Trained in the old ways by his Bavarian forefathers, Trump comes from a long lineage revered for its brave monster hunts throughout the centuries. Here he reveals his ancestors' strategies as written in the ancient *Trump Book of Ghouls*.

A FRANKENSTEIN

A Frankenstein is a creature that is composed of different dead body parts sewn together and then given life by heretical science. People may say, "Frankenstein was the name of the scientist, not the monster." In the time it takes those people to make that observation, the Frankenstein has crushed their skulls. What is important is that the Frankenstein, an abomination of God and men, is pursued until dead.

The lifeless tissue that makes up a Frankenstein's body creates the effect of a lumbering gait. It is not difficult to outrun a Frankenstein. A Frankenstein is easily distracted and startled. It can only focus its half-dead mind on one thing. However, great caution must be exercised, for if it gets a hold, it can keep hold with a deadly grip. For this reason, it is best to avoid fighting a Frankenstein alone. Every man in the village must be roused to a great fervor, pitchforks, bludgeons, and torches in hand, convinced in their rightness to destroy the sad monster.

Fire is the only known method of killing a Frankenstein. Removal of the brain from the rest of the body is also recommended as a safeguard. Even burning and decapitated, a Frankenstein's body may be able to walk and grab for as long as one hour. Be aware and keep a distance until it finally falls. When that happens, make certain both head and body are burned to ashes.

A VAMPIRE

A Vampire is thought to be a lascivious aristocrat which prowls the night for twisted, undead love. For this reason it is to be admired. There is much we can learn from the Vampire, such as projecting powerful psychic desires within the minds of captivated thralls, and maintaining strength, sexual vitality, and smooth hair with an unearthly shimmer until far beyond an age when such traits would be natural.

While legend has put forth that the way to kill a Vampire is with a wooden stake or direct sunlight, the truth is that only decapitation will kill a Vampire. But before you kill it, learn its secrets. Let it drink your blood. This course of action will bestow upon you a long life of untold personal magnetism and worldly success.

A WEREWOLF

A Werewolf is a dumb brute, a man who shape-shifts into a man-wolf under a full moon. A Werewolf can be harmed by wolfsbane and holy artifacts, but only silver to the heart is lethal. Harming a Werewolf is unwise. A Werewolf fearing for its life can kill a hundred men before it tires. Shots are best fired from a great distance, as one scratch from the Werebeast will pass the infliction onto you. Alas, there is no known cure for lycanthropy. To blot out the Werewolf we must work toward a future in which the Dark Arts and Science develop a weapon capable of destroying the moon.

SCIENCE: "IF EINSTEIN WAS SO SMART, WHY WASN'T HE RICH?"

TRUMP VS. A CREATURE FROM THE BLACK LAGOON

"A few years ago at Mar-a-Lago Club, the famous and historic twenty-acre waterfront estate, named by the American Academy of Hospitality Sciences as 'the best private club in the world,' I started getting reports from the workers of a 'fish-man' lurking in the waters near the resort. I knew exactly what we were dealing with—a merman. I went into the hunter chest that I keep at Mar-a-Lago and got out my golden trident. A golden trident is the only known thing that can kill a merman. I went out on the water with George Ross, executive vice president and senior counsel of the Trump Organization, and we spent over 48 hours searching for this thing, and we finally found it.

"When I shone a light on it, it let out an unholy hissing sound and jumped toward us on the boat. It grabbed onto George's arm and nearly yanked it off. Luckily, I rammed the golden trident right into its chest just in time. It let out a death howl and went limp. I pulled its disgusting, slime-covered body onto the boat and George and I brought it onto shore where we burned it."

WHAT TO DO IF YOU HAVE AN ANCIENT AZTEC CURSE PUT ON YOU

The worst people sometimes resort to the worst weapon: curses. The ancient Aztec dark arts have been handed down over the generations, and there's very little you can do to stop them if you don't know what you're doing. Due to his stance on Mexicans, Donald Trump has tangled with his fair share of ancient Aztec curses. Here is his step-by-step guide to dispelling the evil hexes.

1. Construct a pyramid-shaped temple with a westward-facing facade. Sunlight must shine directly through the 24-pound polished gemstone perched in the doorway, creating a luxurious interplay of light and shadow within the antechamber.

2. Perform an incantation to the feathered serpent Quetzalcoatl.

3. Make a blood sacrifice. This may cause trouble, but you must ask yourself: would you rather face our nation's weak justice system, or the damnation of unspeakable forces from the underworld realm of Mictlan?

4. To prevent a curse being recast, close the temple with the seal of the cloud serpent, hewn from puma skulls.

5. Summon a muertos vivientes and cover it with one part red earth consecrated by an Aztec priest, and one part pure snow from a mountain peak. Send the creature forth as your avatar.

6. Wear the sacred headdress of the tlamacazqui order until you are certain the curse has fully dissipated.

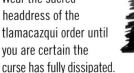

YOUR LIFE

A STUDY IN LOSING

10 Simple Tips To Transform Yourself From A Total Loser To Just A Loser

As president, Donald Trump does not tolerate total losers among the American citizenry. If you are currently a total loser, you need to start remaking yourself today. Here are 10 things you can do right now. If you have your sights on being a Trump-caliber winner, too bad. Only Donald Trump can be that good. You need to focus on becoming a better kind of loser.

1. You are the company you keep. Get rid of all your total-loser friends and surround yourself with only loser friends.

2. Remove all references to your being a total loser from your LinkedIn profile.

3. Get an assistant loser who is a bigger loser than you.

4. Buy a StairMaster and set it for Trump's penthouse level (80 flights) then walk it 20 times per day while chanting "I'm a loser."

5. You may never date a beauty from a classy Eastern European country, but try your luck with Moldova or Azerbaijan.

6. Start saving for a low-end helicopter.

7. Get your assistant an assistant. If your assistant already has an assistant, get her a hotter assistant. If your assistant's assistant is already a 10, make her your assistant and fire the first one for not being hot enough.

8. Call others "total losers" to distance yourself from the stigma.

9. Surround yourself with total bozos to distract you from being a total loser.

10. Stop drinking out of the garden hose.

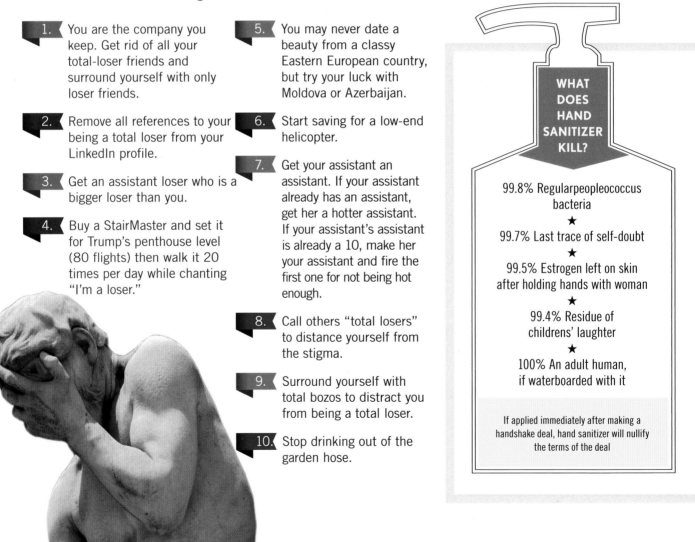

WHAT DOES HAND SANITIZER KILL?

99.8% Regularpeopleococcus bacteria

★

99.7% Last trace of self-doubt

★

99.5% Estrogen left on skin after holding hands with woman

★

99.4% Residue of childrens' laughter

★

100% An adult human, if waterboarded with it

If applied immediately after making a handshake deal, hand sanitizer will nullify the terms of the deal

Politically Correct Term	Trump's Term	Time Saved Using Trump's Term	What Trump Can Accomplish in the Time Saved
African-Americans	The Blacks	0.8 seconds	Make America great again
Undocumented workers	Mexicans	0.5 seconds	Build another wall
Muslims	Terrorists	-0.2 seconds	Actually takes more time, but worth it
Women	Cows	0.1 seconds	Cherish women
LGBTQ community	The Gays	2 seconds	Make love to a beautiful woman
Developmentally disabled	Retards	2.2 seconds	Make fun of some spaz who deserves it
Little people	Midgets	0.6 seconds	Think of new jobs midgets could do
Quds Force	Kurds	0.2 seconds	Berate unfair reporter
Republicans	Crybabies	0.4 seconds	Get hair just right
Democrats	Losers	0.4 seconds	Defeat ISIS
Conservatives	Clowns	0.7 seconds	Confiscate Mideast oil
Liberals	Bozos	0.3 seconds	Order person who desecrated his Walk of Fame star to be tortured
Detainment camps	Fun Zone	1.3 seconds	Give two thumbs up for the cameras

WARNING

POLITICALLY INCORRECT ZONE

INSENSITIVITY AUTHORIZED

TRUMP FACT
Donald Trump enjoys sharing his opinions with others.

Top Trump Tweets

I will never donate blood because I made it and it's mine.

. . .

COMPLETE-DISASTER PREPAREDNESS GUIDE

You never know when complete disaster will strike. Whether it's Jeb Bush's disastrous campaign for the Republican nomination or Obamacare, it's always a good idea to be prepared. In Trump's America, you can rest assured that Trump has thought of every contingency. You can be ready for anything with these easy-to-follow emergency guidelines.

Complete Disaster: Your limo guy is running late
Response: Call your helicopter guy

Complete Disaster: The concierge did not greet you at the hotel
Response: Buy the hotel, tear it down, build a Trump hotel in its place and make billions

Complete Disaster: You spill soup on your tie at a restaurant
Response: Text your assistant and instruct her to buy a new tie and bring it to you. If you can't reach your assistant—day or night—or don't know if she'll do anything you ask of her, you've got the wrong assistant

Complete Disaster: You shake too many hands and are overrun with germs
Response: Surgically remove hands and replace them with golden robot hands

Complete Disaster: You're forced to hear a woman speak for more than one minute
Response: Slip on sunglasses with pictures of Ivanka on the back of the lenses

Complete Disaster: Air conditioning doesn't work
Response: Get a clue

Complete Disaster:
You find yourself in the vicinity of a Black Lives Matter rally
Response: Take cover inside the nearest Trump skyscraper

Complete Disaster: You find yourself in a foreign country
Response: Retrace your steps until you're no longer in a foreign country

Complete Disaster: Your wife is not as hot as she used to be
Response: Release her back into the Siberian hinterlands

OUTDOOR SURVIVAL TIPS

Lost? Look around for a giant building with your name on it.

Mark your trail through wooded areas by lighting several fires so that you know where you've been.

Find the biggest bear you can and shoot him in the face. Now all the other animals know you're at the top of the food chain.

Follow any source of water you find. It will most likely lead you to a town with grocery stores, where Trump Ice spring water is likely sold.

In cases of extreme emergency, your driver or personal assistant can be a source of both food and shelter.

Call up Dante and make a reservation for two tonight. Just because you're outside doesn't mean you shouldn't eat well.

Always remember the clubhouse is near the second hole.

If you get lost in the woods, buy the woods and evict anything that might bite or scratch you.

HOW TO HUNT MAN

Serve an Elegant Dinner
Welcome your guest into your jungle chateau. Offer a lavish meal. Over dinner, calmly explain that you're going to hunt him for sport.

Survey Your Island Estate
Thoroughly sweep the tropical grounds that surround your mansion to be sure it's escape-proof and free of any items that your quarry could, with desperate cunning, fashion into a crude weapon.

Let the Hunt Begin
Use your hunting rifle, of course, but also toy with your prey's mind. Explain to him that you are above the moral code of civilized society, and that his naive devotion to it makes him no better than wild game. Let his faith in man's inherent goodwill be his undoing.

Enjoy Yourself
You've earned this. Having tired of hunting animals, the thrill of tracking and killing a creature with reason is the only thing that offers any kind of challenge. Have fun with it.

ARE YOU IN A TRUMP CASINO HOTEL OR A FEVER DREAM?

Flashing lights and colors are unrealistically intense

Nonsensical, maddening architecture

Feeling of being watched

Demons or Gorns

You'd swear it's 1987 again

You're in a casino that's better than a Trump casino

Trump Casino

Fever Dream

Profuse sweating

Porn stars are buying you drinks

Seemingly bottomless buffet of shrimp

Visceral image of your late father mocking your failure

You're cashing in your winning chips

If you're in the Fever Dream Fantasy Suite at a Trump Casino Resort, you're in both

USA Today, May 21, 2023

Trump: 'Every child deserves to be maybe half as great as me'

President inspires kids to be small percentage of what he's become.

Ruth Anne Dolezal
USA TODAY

NEW YORK — In a stirring speech delivered at Manhattan's Trinity Prep Elementary this morning, President Trump challenged a room full of fifth graders from the city's most wealthy and connected families to be almost

TIMOTHY NADEAU, GETTY IMAGES
President Donald Trump.

as great as himself.

"If you put in the time and work, maybe, and you learn to

be confident at all costs, which is very difficult especially if you have no spine, you can be almost as unstoppable as Trump," Trump said.

He tasked each child to make the most of their opportunities. "With your business connections, which I can tell you pale in comparison to mine, your net worth, which is a fraction of Trump's at best, coupled with the inspiration you take from this incredible speech, maybe, one day, if you put all that together, you'll deserve to be mentioned in the

same sentence as me. Maybe."

Trump stressed that this ideal was something the children could hope for only under the best circumstances. "Worst-case scenario, you'll remain nobodies."

In answer to a girl's question about Mideast peace, Trump complimented her appearance, and expressed optimism that she could possibly achieve sub-Trump greatness one day. "But certainly no more than that," he said.

STORY CONTINUES ON 2A

STATE-BY-STATE 4A   AMERICA'S MARKETS 5B   MARKETPLACE TODAY 5D   PUZZLES 5D   SCREEN CHECK 6D   WEATHER 6A

TRUMP FACT
Everything Trump touches turns to gold. Literally. Please help him. He is starving.

TRUMP THE GAME

Presidential Edition
★ ★ ★

Earn billions,
bed gorgeous women,
and defeat bozos on
your way to the top

"It's not whether you win or lose, but whether you win!"

TRUMP THE GAME
Donald J. Trump

BLOWS CANDY LAND ON ITS ASS!

★ Repeal the Civil Rights Act, win additional property!

★ Start a nuclear war—you win!

★ Includes economic and military policy game cards, 4 Trump President game pieces, and real U.S. dollars confiscated from deported illegals!

★ Use your army to defeat enemy AND allied nations!

★ Makes chess look queer!

Do you possess the leadership skills to be the Winner in Chief? Or, were you born a loser like failed President Barack Obama? Find out as you circle the game board conquering ISIS, creating so many jobs it will make your head spin, and making love to the world's most beautiful women.

7 CHUMPS WHO GOT EXECUTED

Trump knows the death penalty is 100 percent effective at deterring violent crime, and it never kills innocent people by mistake—they're all chumps who deserve it. In Trump's America, a lot more chumps like these will get what's coming to them.

JOHN WINFIELD
Method Lethal injection
What kind of chump was he?
Classless chump

PAUL WARNER POWELL
Method Electric chair
What kind of chump was he?
Chicken-fried chump

CHADWICK BANKS
Method Lethal injection
What kind of chump was he?
Chumpwick Banks

MANUEL PARDO
Method Lethal injection
What kind of chump was he?
Superchump

DAVID ZINK
Method Lethal injection
What kind of chump was he?
He was driving the chump truck

MARVALLOUS KEENE
Method Lethal injection
What kind of chump was he?
A chump who didn't even die right

TRUMP ON FAITH

For all of his tough talk of the Wall, getting rid of Muslims, and the need to rough up protesters from time to time, there is one thing that is very special to Donald Trump: religion.

"I love the Bible and am very close to God, but I've got a few bones to pick with his son. I love Jesus, too, but there are a lot of things I would have done differently. First, I'm not a fan of people who let themselves be crucified. I prefer saviors who win. If I were Jesus, my apostles would be made up of people who were very big in their fields. The top scholars. Who did Jesus have as apostles? Weirdos and lowlifes. This was a bunch of freeloaders, and the church is in a terrible state to this day because of it. Put me in charge of the church and I could fix it in a week. Get the brightest people in there and throw the dummies out. I could make church very successful again—very successful.

"Let's look at everything Jesus ever did: he gave speeches, did some miracles, and then let himself be killed. That's not the life of a winner.

Top Trump Tweets

People say we have problems with race relations in this country. What problems? I've been mentioned by many rappers.

· · ·

David Blaine can do two out of three of those things, but that doesn't make him a savior. I know David. He's a friend of mine and I've seen a lot of his shows. No one knows how to liven up a crowd like David, except maybe for me, I have to be honest with you.

"I'm worth over 8 billion dollars, how much was Jesus worth? Do you really want to take life-investment advice from a nobody? I know business. I know the market. I know deals. Can Jesus say that? Well, you can't ask him because he died.

"When I read the Bible and see where we had all of Jesus's so-called miracles, I have to laugh. I've done what he's done 10 times over. He brought a guy back from the dead. Hey, I've got to tell you: I brought thousands of casinos back from the brink. That's what I do. Jesus never did business with China. The Chinese love me. From what I've been told, they don't like Jesus very much. And for good reason. He was lazy.

"You know, the more I think about it, the more I realize God is a grade-A loser, too. What kind of a schmuck lets his son—who has no talent—run around speaking for him and giving not-so-great advice about giving away all your stuff? When Donald Jr. takes over my companies, he's not going to wander around like a hippie and cure sick people for free, that much I can tell you.

"God couldn't control his brand. He wrote the Bible, but what that book needs is an editor. There were a lot of great Jew characters in the first half, but where did they go? God is a poor writer. And his son was a disappointment.

"Bottom line: Jesus is a lowlife and a wimp who couldn't keep his hair out of his eyes. And God is a lousy boss with communication problems. I am everything they weren't."

JESUS	TRUMP
Gave the "sermon on the mount"	Has spoken to much bigger crowds
Spawned a world religion with over a billion faithful	Has 8 billion dollars
Turned water into wine	Turned failed investments into world-class properties worth much more than water or wine
Healed lepers	Many people have come into Trump casinos losers, but left winners
Suffered on the cross	Suffered relentless attacks from the media during 2016 campaign
Said, "Love your neighbor as yourself"	Said, "I get along with everybody, not just my neighbors. Jesus was thinking small."

The Trump Family Heirloom Bible

A childhood gift from his mother, Donald Trump's Holy Bible is always at his side.

HOLY BIBLE

Special modifications he's made over the years make it a cherished keepsake.

The New York Times

"All the News That's Fit to Print"

Late Edition
Today, intervals of clouds and sunshine, quite mild, high 60. Tonight, partly cloudy, mild, low 49. Tomorrow, clouds and sun, quite mild, high 62. Weather map, Page B12.

VOL. CLXXIII . . . No. 70,077+ © 2025 The New York Times   NEW YORK, MONDAY, JANUARY 6, 2025 $3.00

'THE FOREIGN WOMEN WHO DO MY SKIN TREATMENTS ARE TALKING SHIT ABOUT ME AND IT ENDS NOW'

Major Address
President Trump moments before excoriating the "dishonest beauticians who are probably insulting me." Full transcript on Page A15.

PHILIP McGENTRY / THE NEW YORK TIMES

NEWS ANALYSIS

Deep Wounds In Long-Standing Language Gap

By ALLEN D. KIRKPATRICK

President Donald Trump has often leveled charges against the workers at the Manhattan salon where he pays for skin, hair, and nails treatments, accusing them of talking about him and laughing at him in a language he cannot understand.

With his address to the nation tonight, he indicated a new phase of his strained relationship with the salon workers. He is expected to introduce tough new proposals to end the threat: the creation of an Upper West Side Asian-language task force readied for deployment at a moment's notice to any salon where the staff is saying unflattering things about the president; and emergency funding for a "translator thing like they have on Star Trek."

Mr. Trump may call for military tribunals for beauticians, cosmetologists, manicurists, or waxers suspected of making unflattering comments near him.

Continued on Page A14

TRUMP REBUKES ASIAN SALON MANICURISTS

President's Strongest Language on the Issue

By GERALD LA FAZIA

WASHINGTON—In a special address to the nation today from the East Room of the White House, President Trump offered his strongest language yet against the Asian women who do his skin treatments. He has singled out the group in several speeches recently, as well as in pieces of legislation he has urged Congress to enact into law.

"I've seen it happen, and you know what I'm talking about," he said. "The short one gestures at the other one. They share a laugh. Then the one doing the nails joins in. Now they're all laughing, and saying things in Chinese or Japanese or whatever it is." Trump pledged that by 2030, America will "make it stop, and make it stop now."

Continued on Page A15

DISCOVERING THE MOST AUTHENTIC PIZZA IN NEW YORK'S TRUMP TOWER

Trump Tower native Donald Trump has sampled cuisine from all over Trump Tower. But of course, when you're in Trump Tower, the most important local cuisine is the pizza!

For the best Trump-Tower pizza, Trump recommends Trump Tower Pizzeria. Their recipe dates back to the first settlers of the Tower in 1983, when the owner arrived on the first boat to dock at Trump Tower harbor. Nestled on the Trump Tower mezzanine level, it boasts fresh trumpmatoes grown on the Trump Tower rooftop garden, seasoned with herbs grown fresh in Trumpalonia, and topped with cheese made from pure, grass-fed Trumpmilk. Try it next time you visit Trump Tower!

HOW TO HAVE A DECENT VACATION WITHOUT SPENDING A MILLION DOLLARS

- Use $50 bills as napkins instead of $100 bills
- Don't buy the country you visit
- Limit yourself to one souvenir car
- Cut your expenses in half by getting a divorce
- Bring peanut butter and jelly sandwiches
- Yacht surf
- Spend lavishly, then sue everyone involved
- Cut employee pay leading up to vacation
- Figure out what "camping" is
- Only tip in ass slaps

YOU ARE WHERE YOU LIVE

In Trump's America you need to know where the undesirables are. It's as easy as looking at their address. Here's a handy list.

Unit	*Bore*
Apartment	*Loser*
Garden apartment	*Schmuck*
Basement	*Lowlife*
Finished attic	*Goon*
Unfinished attic	*Slob*
Parent's basement	*Sad Sack*
Yurt	*Lummox*
Tent	*Rapist*
Shitty tent	*Mexican rapist*
Non-Trump condo	*Nobody*
Vacationing at an Airbnb	*Geek*
Live in a car	*Clown*
Live in a car but the car is a limo	*Bozo*
Motel	*Chump*
Single-family home	*Bumpkin*
Bungalow	*Moron*
Shack	*Dumbo*
Barn	*Pig*
Cave	*Dope*
Cottage	*Girly Man*
Geodesic dome	*Nutcase*
Igloo	*Sissy*
Log cabin	*Zero*
McMansion	*Wannabe*
Tree house	*Nincompoop*
Townhouse	*Lightweight*
Garage	*Terrorist*
Houseboat	*Quitter*

HOW TO TELL IF YOUR YACHT SALESMAN IS A NOBODY

Doesn't have his own yacht salesman

⚙

Offers complimentary champagne in plastic flutes

⚙

Can't remember which of your kids has which mother

⚙

Asks if you want the yacht in a color other than gold

⚙

Doesn't offer you the model with the helipad

⚙

Uses "affordable" as a selling point

⚙

Doesn't throw in a guest yacht upon purchase

⚙

Has never had the honor of being a guest
on Saddam Hussein's yacht

⚙

Can't name the official yacht mascot, Sir Yachtsworth

⚙

Can't tell the difference between a water 8 and a land 9

HOW TO HANG YOURSELF WITH A TRUMP-BRAND SIGNATURE TIE

 1. Select a tie from the Donald J. Trump Neckwear Collection, available at only the finest retailers.

 2. Cross the wide end of the tie over the narrow end right at the level of the "Made in China" tag.

 3. Pass the wide end around the front and reflect on the failures that have brought you to this moment. Bad business deals? Unlucky in love? It certainly wasn't your taste in neckwear.

 4. While you bring the wide end up through the loop, remember that even at the end of your life, it's still important to enjoy the little things, such as this tie's smooth, exquisite silk.

 5. As you yank up on the tie to end your small life, take solace in the fact that your lifeless body will be both stylish and elegant, as ready for a boardroom meeting as it is for a night on the town.

WHEN TO OFFER YOUR WIFE TO TRUMP

Melania's 50th birthday

President's Day

Flag Day

4th of July

During a debate to punctuate a great point

Before sealing a real-estate contract with Trump

When you need to throw off suspicion of Muslim activity

During sex with someone else's wife

When your yacht is sinking off the coast of one of Trump's private islands

When you, your wife, and Trump are lost in the Arctic and Trump needs warmth

The moment you can no longer be the provider, CEO, and multibillionaire president she needs

Top Trump Tweets

I'm sad = I'm a loser. Depression is baloney.

. . .

THE POWERFUL TRUMP SLEEP SYSTEM

Donald Trump is renowned for sleeping only four hours per night yet having boundless energy during the day. How does he do it? With his powerful Trump-brand sleep system: a proprietary method developed by Trump to create more vitality, increase productivity, and kick sleep's ass.

TRUMP'S SECRET STRATEGIES FOR 4 HOURS OF SLEEP

☾ Takes a six-hour-per-day power nap
☾ Hires people to sleep for him
☾ Powers down while Melania speaks
☾ Licenses his name and image to other people's sleep
☾ Sleeps across three beds, for a total of 12 hours of sleep
☾ Conserves energy during the day by having a team of interns perform the functions of many of his vital organs
☾ Sleeps on private jet crossing back and forth over the international dateline
☾ Goes by winner's time

TRUMP'S POWER SLEEP SUIT

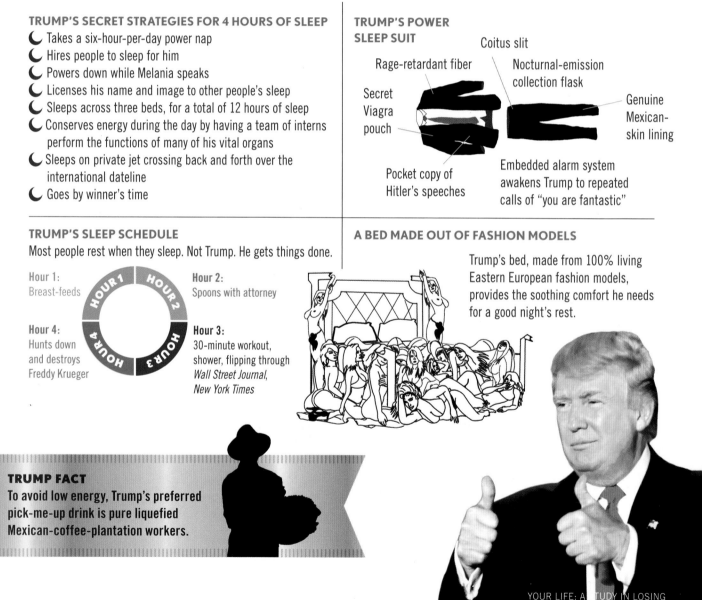

- Coitus slit
- Rage-retardant fiber
- Nocturnal-emission collection flask
- Secret Viagra pouch
- Genuine Mexican-skin lining
- Pocket copy of Hitler's speeches
- Embedded alarm system awakens Trump to repeated calls of "you are fantastic"

TRUMP'S SLEEP SCHEDULE

Most people rest when they sleep. Not Trump. He gets things done.

HOUR 1 · HOUR 2 · HOUR 3 · HOUR 4

Hour 1: Breast-feeds

Hour 2: Spoons with attorney

Hour 3: 30-minute workout, shower, flipping through *Wall Street Journal, New York Times*

Hour 4: Hunts down and destroys Freddy Krueger

A BED MADE OUT OF FASHION MODELS

Trump's bed, made from 100% living Eastern European fashion models, provides the soothing comfort he needs for a good night's rest.

TRUMP FACT
To avoid low energy, Trump's preferred pick-me-up drink is pure liquefied Mexican-coffee-plantation workers.

Circle the game board to escape Dad's creepy comments about how sexy you look!

"It's not whether you win or lose, but whether you win!"

TRUMP
THE GAME

FAMILY GAME NIGHT HAS NEVER BEEN SO AWKWARD!

TRUMP
THE GAME
Ivanka Edition

You're a model, CEO of your own business, and the daughter of a multi-billionaire who can't stop talking about how he'd date you if you weren't his daughter.

Step inside the heels of Ivanka Trump as you walk, run, and jump anywhere to evade your dad's weird compliments. You might take your career back two spaces because his unseemly glances give your staff the heebie-jeebies. You might draw a Confrontation Card and insist he not tell reporters how hot he thinks you are. Either way, you lose!

Places to Hide:
Trunk of Bentley • As mannequin in display window • Dangle from the Trump Tower penthouse window

Inappropriate Features
• Gain 1 pound, lose a present at Christmas
• Change the entrance code to your residence, spin again • Refuse to model Miss Universe gown for father, go to room
• Move quietly— don't wake him up!
• Wear your baggy Wharton sweatshirt to avert his gaze

YES, YOU CAN DELIVER A MOVING EULOGY WHILE STILL CALLING THEM OUT FOR THE MISTAKES THEY MADE

TRUMP'S TIPS

☑ Mention their accomplishments and how they won't last. Gleaming skyscrapers and perfectly manicured fairways endure for ages. But whoever died likely had neither in their name, so it should be stated that whatever they did with their life was not that impressive.

☑ Assess whether you would have hired them. A person's life is their ultimate resumé. If this person was not a good hire, now's the time to bring that up.

☑ Criticize the suit they chose to be buried in. The suit you're buried in should be the nicest one you ever wear. There's no excuse for anything else. You should be able to tell just by peeking. Flip over the collar and read the label.

☑ Acknowledge it's a sad time, because whoever died could have lived a much better life. Did they make over a billion dollars? Did they ever get elected president? Were they Donald Trump? No. Make this point clearly and loudly.

☑ For every bad quality you mention about the person, say one good thing about their daughter's appearance.

CREATING MEANINGFUL, POSITIVE CHANGE THROUGH CYBERBULLYING

Just a few short years ago, if someone was a no-talent bum, there was no way to let them know. Today, the Internet makes exposing gutless frauds a fast and efficient part of everyday life. But if they bully you, how can you take the scumbags down, call them out for their lies, and have a lasting social impact?

NEVER GIVE UP

Hit attackers back as hard as you can. Attack their unsuccessful business, their hideous face, or their sow-like weight. Do they have $8 billion? Do they have a helicopter? Probably not. Are they associated with a poorly performing business or entertainment property? Most likely. These are important data points you can offer to the conversation and elevate the dialog. It's not over until your attacker comes crawling to you, begging for forgiveness, admitting they were wrong, and conceding you are their moral superior in every way.

DOES CYBERBULLYING GO FAR ENOUGH?

While cyberbullying can often result in positive change, it sometimes isn't enough. There are times when you must use other means, such as directing media attention to how big of a jackass your opponent is, or giving out your attacker's personal phone number or home address, so that others can rally to your defense.

POWER MOVES TO SILENCE INTERNET TROLLS

Don't just take on the troll, take on his whole family, organization, demographic, and race.

Start a real-estate empire, buy the property they rent, and then evict them.

Call a telecom CEO and ask him to shut down the Internet in the troll's tristate area.

Post a picture of your computer to Instagram to show the troll how much better your computer is than theirs. If it's not a very good computer, buy the best, most expensive computer on the market.

Buy Twitter, find the troll's information, post it to an ISIS message board, then have them arrested for conspiracy to commit terrorism.

Charter a private jet to the troll's parents' house, then call from the parents' phone so the troll can hear the sound of you fucking their mom.

Paste that "what a clown" tweet you copied and saved three years ago.

Buy a Trump-brand Signature tie for every negative comment you get, then Instagram photos of your magnificent ties until the troll breaks down crying over the stark inferiority of their own life.

Top Trump Tweets

If I were a rapist—and I'm not saying that I am—my victims would be very happy, believe me.

• • •

WHAT TO DO IF YOUR CHILD IS A CYBERBULLYING VICTIM

★ Help your child understand that their cyberbully makes some very good points

★ Explain that your child's pain means they're a nerd—a valuable lesson to learn in life

★ Use tough love—if you overhear your child complaining about being cyerbullied, punch your child in the face

★ Stop having children who are nerds

---

3 STEPS TO PUTTING A STOP TO UNFAIR INTERNET COMMENTS

1. STOP cyberattacks preemptively by blindly insulting anyone and everyone on the Internet

2. STOP cyberbullying and then start it again with an even better target

3. STOP cruel, demeaning, or hateful attacks online by sending them through traditional mail

HOW TO AVOID GETTING SUED BY THE PRESIDENT

WILL THE PRESIDENT SUE YOU?

He might. From his seat of executive power in the White House, Donald Trump will use every advantage to make America great again, including, if necessary, suing you.

KNOW YOUR RIGHTS

Trump has the best lawyers. They know every tool of the legal system and how to use each one with surgical precision to bring you to heel, bankrupt you, or simply drag you through the courts for years until you're a soulless shell of your former self with no memory of the innocent bliss that was once your pitiful life.

It's important to remember that Donald Trump is the victim here. You are the defendant. Whatever your future offense, there's only one person to blame: yourself.

SIMPLE TIPS TO AVOID BEING SUED BY PRESIDENT TRUMP

There's no way to guarantee the president won't sue you. But you can decrease the likelihood with these helpful hints:

✓ When speaking of the president, be sure to use one of these acceptable adjectives:
- Terrific
- Amazing
- Incredible
- Very good
- Very nice

✓ Refrain from using any of the president's registered catchphrases:
- "You're fired"
- "Make America great again"
- "Complete disaster"
- "Billions"
- "Moron"
- "China"

✓ Don't disagree with Donald Trump.

✓ Don't write a letter to Donald Trump.

✓ Chant, "Trump! Trump! Trump!"

✓ Never initiate eye contact. And if you do, never break it.

✓ Don't marry Donald Trump.

✓ Don't do business with Donald Trump.

✓ Live on a life raft in international waters outside the known boundary of any recognized legal jurisdiction.

✓ Be directly related to Donald Trump.

✓ Have Donald Trump's blood type and be there when he needs your blood.

✓ Stop spreading the lies of science.

✓ Get your facts straight.

✓ Just shut up.

✓ Live in the sewers and emerge only under the cover of darkness to scavenge the filth of the street to survive.

RE: ACTION THAT WILL LIKELY BE TAKEN IF CURRENT SITUATION NOT REMEDIED — CEASE & DESIST

DEAR SIR/MADAME:

I REPRESENT DONALD TRUMP, THE HIGHLY RESPECTED BUSINESS EXECUTIVE, CHAIRMAN OF THE TRUMP ORGANIZATION, SUCCESSFUL REAL-ESTATE MAGNATE, POPULAR REALITY TELEVISION STAR (THE APPRENTICE, CELEBRITY APPRENTICE), PRESIDENT, AND SOLE OWNER OF THE REGISTERED TRADEMARKS TRUMP®, "MAKE AMERICA GREAT AGAIN®," "YOU'RE FIRED™," AND "BIG LEAGUE®."

IT HAS COME TO MY ATTENTION THAT YOU ARE CURRENTLY READING "TRUMP'S AMERICA: THE COMPLETE LOSER'S GUIDE," A BOOK WHICH WAS NOT AUTHORIZED BY MR. TRUMP NOR HIS SIGNATORY COMPANIES. FURTHER, THIS BOOK MISREPRESENTS AND MALIGNS MY CLIENT'S RECOGNIZED TRUMP® BRANDS, AND THEREFORE CAUSES IRREPARABLE DAMAGE TO HIS BUSINESS AND HIS STANDING IN THE PUBLIC EYE. CONSEQUENTLY, I DEMAND THAT YOU IMMEDIATELY CEASE AND DESIST FROM READING "TRUMP'S AMERICA: THE COMPLETE LOSER'S GUIDE," AND, FURTHER, THAT YOU STRIKE FROM MEMORY ANY ARTICLES, MISSTATED FACTS, ERRANT OPINIONS, OR MISLEADING IMAGERY OF MY CLIENT OR HIS PRODUCTS THAT YOU MAY HAVE SEEN IN THE BOOK.

IN ADDITION, I DEMAND YOU CEASE AND DESIST FROM ENJOYING THIS BOOK IN ANY WAY. BOOKS, WITH THE EXCEPTION OF BOOKS OF BUSINESS ADVICE WRITTEN BY MR. TRUMP, ARE DAMAGING TO THE TRUMP NAME AND REPUTATION. THE READING OF BOOKS LEADS TO FEELINGS OF ENJOYMENT, MERRIMENT, AND SOMETIMES LAUGHTER. THESE THINGS ARE UNACCEPTABLE TO MR. TRUMP. LAUGHTER IS NOT A PROTECTED RIGHT UNDER THE U.S. CONSTITUTION. DONALD TRUMP DOES NOT TOLERATE LAUGHTER NOR DOES HE HIMSELF ENGAGE IN IT. THESE ACTIONS ARE THEREFORE WITHOUT AUTHORIZATION OR PERMISSION FROM MR. TRUMP. YOUR EXPRESSION OF FEELING IS IRREPARABLY HARMING MR. TRUMP. THE NAME TRUMP®, PROTECTED BY U.S TRADEMARK REGISTRATION NO.6453ZB347, ENTITLES MR. TRUMP TO RECOVER (I) FINANCIAL DAMAGES (II) COURT INJUNCTION, AND (III) LEGAL FEES IN THE EVENT THAT YOU LAUGH AT HIM.

MR. TRUMP IS VERY SERIOUS ABOUT PROTECTING THE GOODWILL OF THE TRUMP® BRAND AND HAS ENGAGED ME TO TAKE APPROPRIATE AND IMMEDIATE ACTION TO HALT YOUR INFRINGEMENT UPON HIS RIGHTS. IN THE INTEREST OF AVOIDING A VERY COSTLY LITIGATION PROCESS, I AM OFFERING YOU THIS SINGULAR OPPORTUNITY TO AMEND THIS MATTER BY PROVIDING US WITH WRITTEN CONFIRMATION THE SUBSEQUENT:

(I) YOU WILL STOP READING "TRUMP'S AMERICA: THE COMPLETE LOSER'S GUIDE." (II) YOU WILL NOT SAY "TRUMP®." (III) YOU WILL NOT LOOK AT TRUMP. (IV) YOU WILL OBEY TRUMP.

I AWAIT YOUR COMPLIANT RESPONSE.

KINDEST PROFESSIONAL REGARDS,

KENNETH C. GRAYSON

Top Trump Tweets

Sesame Street is prime New York real estate that's wasted on multicultural, lower-middle-class puppets.

...

WHAT'S NEXT

"IT WAS AN HONOR FOR YOU"

BEHOLD A MONUMENT FIT FOR A TRUMP

The always forward-thinking Donald Trump has already begun construction on a national monument to celebrate his presidency. The Trump Monument is an eight-story abstract rendition of the president encased in an impenetrable tungsten-carbide alloy with a gleaming, armored exterior. As awe-inspiring as this monument will be on the outside, what's inside is even more impressive.

STANDING PROUD AND STRONG
The structure's endoskeleton is made of carbon nanofiber–reinforced, military-grade titanium for superior structural strength and durability. Connected to this framework are thousands of hydraulics, pistons, and actuators to manipulate the monument's many powerful appendages. Of particular note are its finely articulated hands, which are capable of both removing a man's cap before the national anthem and tearing a battleship in half.

AMBULATORY AND COMBAT-READY
When not standing atop its granite pedestal, the Trump Monument is fully mobile, on land and in the air. In times of war or civil unrest, Trump himself will enter the monument and pilot it to defend loyal Americans. Outfitted with concealed 800-kilowatt lasers as well as shoulder-mounted nuclear-missile launchers, the monument is fit to lead our armies into battle or, if necessary, annihilate an American city, securing President Trump's legacy for millennia to come.

HOW TO PROPERLY SALUTE THE TRUMP MONUMENT

In time, all American citizens will be invited by special presidential edict to salute the Trump Monument, as well as any of the other monuments to Donald Trump that will surely be erected in countless cities and townships across the land in the coming years. But what is the appropriate protocol by which fealty is shown to a great leader's bust, statue, or obelisk? Only the most respectful and dignified display of abject acclaim will be acceptable. Each citizen has a responsibility to understand the proper salute form, so you'd better start practicing at home now.

REMOVE HEADGEAR
Within 100 yards of any token or likeness of Trump, or within visible distance of any statue or monument to Trump that is over 100 feet tall, headgear must be removed and placed over the heart. While headgear is decorously held in this manner, walking, talking, or continuing affairs of the day will not be tolerated within a period of not less than one hour. For due respect to be shown a monument in a moving column or parade, this salute must be rendered as the monument approaches and held until it has passed.

BOW HEAD
You confer the proper regard for a Trump monument and everything it stands for by solemnly lowering your head and looking away from any Trump monument or legion of soldiers that may be marching alongside it or in front of it. Spectators may only raise their heads within sight of a Trump monument if so ordered by a soldier, other military, police, or government authority, or by the monument itself or the pilot within it.

GENUFLECT
Dropping to one's knee as if in worship is a gesture of humility and reverence in the face of your superiors. This is the salute required if a Trump monument addresses you directly, either by loudspeaker or with targeting-computer warning.

HONOR TRUMP'S ACHIEVEMENTS
Donald Trump has given more to America than he can ever expect to receive in return. He has accepted this fact, selflessly. But as a beneficiary of his magnanimous leadership, you must show the proper gratitude. While basking in the presence of any of his monuments, take a moment to silently reflect on the gifts he has bestowed upon all of us, such as the many hours of outstanding reality television, and his mercy, for he has the power and the right to obliterate you on the spot with his monument's lasers.

TWEET
Be sure to capture for all time the inspiring moment of your encounter with a Trump monument by taking a photo with the monument and tweeting it to

@realDonaldTrump with an accompanying remark about how incredible he is. No selfies permitted unless you are an 8 or above.

SCORN A TRUMP MONUMENT, GO TO PRISON
Improperly saluting any Trump monument will be punishable by 30 years in prison, a fine of no less than $10,000, and/or registry on the enemy kill list. Defacing a Trump monument in any way will be punishable by immediate stepping-on by the Trump Monument.

VISIT THE GIFT SHOP
Purchase souvenirs of your life-changing confrontation with a Trump monument at one of the official gift shops found at every Trump Tribute Center. Pictures and stories are great, but why not take home a small stuffed Trump Monument doll for a special child in your life? (It shoots fun toy missiles!) Or a Trump Signature refrigerator magnet? All proceeds will go to support the creation of more Trump monuments. (Minimum purchase $1,000.)

How Will Trump Age In Office?

Being president takes its toll. Most of our leaders age visibly from the heavy burden of command. How will Trump look after eight years in office?

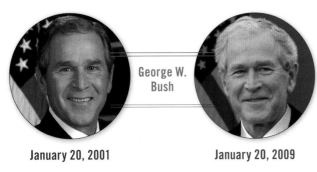

George W. Bush

January 20, 2001   January 20, 2009

Barack Obama

January 20, 2009   January 20, 2017

Donald Trump

January 20, 2017   January 20, 2025

How Could Trump Keep Being President?

★ Run as "Donald Tromp" with a fake mustache

★ Run as vice president, then kill the president

★ Declare the executive branch bankrupt, then acquire the office in a leveraged buyout by the Trump Organization.

★ No one wants to follow Trump as the next president, so Trump will reluctantly agree to stay in office.

★ Reveal that Trump can legally continue to be president because he was technically never president in the first place. He was merely a majority shareholder in a temporary presidential holding company.

★ Yell very loudly until the next president caves and gives Trump what he wants

★ Act like it's his first day as president, and act incredulous when anyone tries to insist otherwise

★ Demand a do-over

★ Create a golem to lead, like Chuckie

★ Build a wall around the White House

★ Demonstrate that he can destroy a planet by nuking Mars

★ Draft and sign Declaration of Presidence

★ Purchase the White House, become new president's landlord

★ Make rigged putting-green bet with new president for control of country

★ Threaten to poison Trump Ice spring water unless demands are met

★ Arrange for Ivanka to marry the new president

★ Program Trumpbot to win next election, transfer consciousness into Trumpbot

★ Swap bodies with new president

★ Purchase all the land in America, rent it to the government

★ Demoralize new president with consistent put-downs

What's next for Trump?

After he's made America great again, when he's remade it into Trump's America—or maybe when he's just had enough—Donald Trump will finally, eventually, leave the White House. What will his next great calling be? Only time will tell. For the rest of us, whether losers, lowlifes, or lightweights, we will continue to stand in his shadow, blinded by the resplendent spectacle of Donald Trump, sure to be the greatest *former* president the world has ever known.

Flip White House for 300% profit after cost of renovations

Devote self to new charity, Habitat for the Haves

Become bad-will ambassador

"Forget" to release Bill Maher from Guantánamo Bay

Give away all worldly possessions and devote life to comforting the sick

Divorce Melania, marry self

Finally get down to writing his seventh memoir

Admonish the nation for not sending flowers and a thank-you note

Create island nation where incest is legal

Lead resistance of human survivors to win back Earth from the machines

Mutate into a shark and dominate the seas

Fly to outer space in a rocketship hewn from the bones of Mexicans

Top Trump Tweets

RT: @veklyfg92879 donald trumpzz the best EVER!!! awesooem!! #America #RealTrump #Greatest

• • •

TRUMP

INTERNATIONAL HOTEL & TOWER®

NEW YORK

A NOTE TO FUTURE HISTORIAN HACKS WHO WANT TO MAKE A QUICK BUCK
BY DRAGGING A GREAT PRESIDENT THROUGH THE MUD
by Donald J. Trump

I have something to say to you historians who I know will be
dying to take me down a peg with a big smear job after I'm
President. You'll try to pass it off as "scholarship." But I've
got news for you people: no one is buying it. People are going
to know that everything you write about me is absolute garbage.

You'll say I said the wrong thing, or that I was politically
incorrect when I did that one thing. Or maybe you'll say all the
great things I'll do as President are somehow not great!

No matter what you say, here's what's going to happen. By the
end of my presidency, America is going to love me. They're going
to be so happy. And great. People will be sick and tired of
being so great and happy and getting rid of all the bad things.

My legacy is going to be fabulous. Just incredible.

I'm going to pull this country from the brink of disaster where
Obama left it, and give it victories, and self-respect, and all
the great things. Terrorism, immigrants, Muslims, the scumbags
from MSNBC. You'll never hear from them again.

These are facts, and whatever you're going to write will be
something else - I don't know what. You will be totally
dishonest, that much I can tell you. And why would you do that?
It's because you're despicable people. Just horrible. The worst.
You're probably not doing very well in your historian job.
You're a little history teacher who works at a little
schoolhouse, who gets paid - what, maybe forty thousand dollars?
You've got a long way to go before you're going to earn anyone's
respect, believe me.

The things you'll write about me in your little history books
will be very unfair, and they will not be true. Not a single
word. But it doesn't matter because nobody cares. Nobody will
read your books. They'll read mine. And that's why you'll come
after me.

So sad.

[signature]